W9-DHT-490

My Remembers

A Black Sharecropper's
Recollections of the Depression

My Remembers

A Black Sharecropper's Recollections of the Depression

Eddie Stimpson, Jr. ("Sarge")

Introduction by James W. Byrd
Foreword by Frances Wells
Illustrated by Burnice
Breckenridge

University of North Texas Press
Denton, Texas

©1996, Eddie Stimpson, Jr.

Manufactured in the United States of America
All rights reserved

10 9 8 7 6 5 4 3 2 1

Requests for permission to reproduce material from this work should
be sent to:
Permissions
University of North Texas Press
PO Box 13856
Denton TX 76203

The paper used in this book meets the minimum requirements of the
American National Standard for Permanence of Paper for Printed
Library Materials, Z39.48.1984.

Library of Congress Cataloging-in-Publication Data

Stimpson, Eddie, 1929-
My remembers : a Black sharecropper's recollections of the
Depression / by Eddie Stimpson, Jr. ("Sarge") ; introduction by James
Byrd; illustrated by Burnice Breckenridge.
p.   cm.
Includes index.
ISBN 0-929398-98-X (cloth : alk. paper)
1. Stimpson, Eddie, 1929-   . 2. Afro-Americans—Texas—
Plano Region—Biography. 3. Sharecroppers—Texas—Plano Region—
Biography. 4. Depressions—1929—Texas—Plano Region. 5. Farm
life—Texas—Plano Region—History—20th century. 6. Plano Region
(Tex.)—Social conditions. I. Title.
F394.P62S75   1995
976.4'555—dc20   95-33312
[B]   CIP

Cover design by Amy Layton

Contents

Foreword

I first became involved with this project in 1990, when I planned to tape oral interviews with Eddie Stimpson, Jr., (known to me as "Sarge") for a sociological study. One of the chapters which I had researched and written for a book sponsored by the Friends of the Plano Public Library—*Plano Texas: The Early Years* (Wolfe City, Texas: Hennington Publishing Company, 1985)—was on farming. It was my favorite, but I was painfully aware that it was told entirely from the point of view of the white landowner. I had searched for, but never found, an account written by a black farmer, and I despaired of ever getting another point of view. Getting to know Sarge through work on another project was a fulfillment of my dream, and our work together became a central personal project for me, with many of my family members getting caught up in the excitement of the work.

During a pre-interview session designed to let him know the types of questions I would be asking, Sarge asked if I would like him to write up the material instead. I was surprised, but said that would be fine. Back he came next week with a yellow legal pad covered with writing—no punctuation, no paragraphing, and spelling largely phonetic—but lively and informative, full of the drama and rhythm of his life. We read through it together, Sarge deciphering the words I could not read, and later I typed it up.[1]

For three years after that, the tape recorder was forgotten, and Sarge came by my house on Mondays at 9:00 A.M. unless I was busy or he was going fishing. When we thought we were finished with the story of Sarge's life, we began going through the whole thing line by line, clarifying, correcting, subtracting a phrase, or adding even as much as a page or chapter, but always careful to maintain the unique style of Sarge's own way of getting things said.[2] After months and months of that process, my granddaughter Erin Cone came home from college and put the manuscript on the computer. We continued to record revisions and additions, determined that the wording remain entirely Sarge's own. Only once did I add a word, and my daughter Nancy Warder caught it immediately. "Mama, you added that word," she said. "Sarge didn't say that." And out came the word "gabardine" to describe Miss Ami's elegant pants. I never tried to insert a word again.

For Sarge, the reason for writing his story was to pass it along to his grandchildren. But as the work took shape, I began to realize that the narrative had wider significance. I approached the Collin County Historical Commission during one of our meetings and the members were immediately supportive of the project. Our chairperson, Lolissa Moores, contacted the University of North Texas Press, whose editor invited her to send the manuscript. This book is the result of that long process.

Eddie Stimpson, Jr., has fulfilled a long-standing dream by writing up the memories of his early years for his descendants. In doing so he has given all of us a glimpse of rural black family life during the Depression, which is largely lacking in our history books. He gives an account of his youth which is factual, detailed, and vivid.

He was born in 1929; his youth covered the Great Depression and World War II, a time of trauma and great change for everyone in the country. He grew up in an area ten miles west of Plano, Texas (but in the Plano school district), which was known for its fertile soil and its stable farm life, carried on generation after generation by descendants of the first white settlers.

The black families had also developed a pattern of continuity. Eddie's father was a sharecropper who followed in the footsteps of two members of the extended famley, one a Drake and one a Stimpson, who, instead of being content to be mere day laborers, sharecropped extensively on either side of Preston Road, using their own teams and equipment.

The Depression was rough for everyone in the Plano area. Until 1929, the banks were glad to lend money so the farmers could make a crop. After the crash, the banks were reluctant to make such loans and farmers had difficulty saving harvest money for that purpose. After cotton went down to four cents a pound in 1932, it brought an average of only ten dollars an acre. Still and all, farm life was generally better than life in town. The farmers, white and black, at least had food from their gardens to eat, to can, and to share with their town relatives when they went to visit.

Eddie Stimpson's story of his life during the Depression and the war years that followed it, begins with an overview called "My Growing Up Days." He then adds more detail on a subject by subject basis. He writes with imagery, rhythm, and an ability to convey emotion which sometimes approaches the poetic. I puzzled over the source of this gift until I realized that his natural talent had been shaped and enriched by his lifelong reading of the scriptures, particularly the Psalms. It has been a rare privilege to have had the opportunity to help with this account.

Frances Wells, longtime Plano resident

---

[1]Editor's note: In preparing this book for publication, I have relied on Frances Wells's original typed manuscript, along with a disk copy she later sent me which was made by yet another person. As the punctuation is largely Wells's rather than Stimpson's, I have corrected that without hesitation. The spelling was a different matter. As an editor, I am ordinarily strive for accuracy or, when an author is adamant about an idiosyncratic spelling, grammar, or punctuation pattern, I at least ask for consistency. In this case, that did not work. The author used such a variety of spellings for some words that it would have been confusing to the reader to be confronted with all of them.

"Family," for instance, was spelled "faimly," "faimley," "famley," and "famly," in addition to the proper spelling. To always change it to the proper spelling seemed to me to be tampering with the spontaneity and character of the work. To leave them all as they were in the manuscript also did not seem right, as some of the misspellings could actually have been errors by the typist, as could the "proper" spellings. One solution to the problem has been to make the spellings conform to the author's most frequent spelling pattern. In the case of "family," then, in this book it is "famley." In other cases, I have let stand two or three varieties of the same word.

I want to make it clear that my "tampering" should not be taken as a judgment of Stimpson's writing ability. On the contrary, I was captivated by his writing style, and wanted to make sure that my editing did not interfere with either the story or the storyteller's way of telling it. Stimpson's writing reflects a unique blend of spoken and written language skills, and whatever changes I have made were designed to help the reader capture the full flavor of Stimpson's narratives.

[2]Editor's note: Frances Wells has stated that Stimpson's writing style became more "polished" during the time they were working on the manuscript. He began working with a dictionary before he got to her house, so that there were fewer spelling errors in the later chapters. His syntax and use of verb tenses became more regular, also. As the final organization of the book does not conform to the order in which Stimpson wrote the chapters, the careful reader will notice some inconsistencies in the overall "voice" of *My Remembers*.

Acknowledgments

It bother me to even think that I could not or would not be able to send out one of the thing that I have built my life upon and that is to be grateful. I wish to send all my thanks to those who have made this book possible by giving me the support I need, and my apologies to those I may miss naming.

First of all I wish to thank Frances Wells for the many hours we sit together in her dinnen room with paper all over the table while she tried to stumble over my bad hand writing and spelling. She finally got the hang of my writing and could read it better than I. I all way say I can't understand my own writing once it get cold.

Secondly, my thanks goes out to Erin Cone who spent hours away from her own studies, some time half the night, typing and staring into the computer until the key and word began to run together.

Thirdly, to Lolissa Moores and her husband who encourage me to send this script to a publisher and refuse to give up when one turn it down. And to T. V. Drake, who is now decease, but incourage me to take a chance. He believed it would be good because someone, someday, might want to know how life really was in my early years of the Depression.

To my uncle A. J. Stimpson who furnish a lot of information about my folk. Since he is my father brother he could pin point some of the event that taken place. Thanks to all my docent friends at the Heritage Farmstead where I volunteer, who continues to incourage me to keep up the good work.

To my aunt Bessie Davis who furnish information on my mother side of the famley. She is my mother sister.

To Pastor Charles and Debby Leach, from New Life Bible Institution in Pleasant Grove, who offer prayer each day at Bible Study for me and the success of the book.

To Betty Neal, R.N., who monitor my health each day.

A special thanks to my niece Brenda Brooks for pulling some of my stories together. Thanks to my daughter, Donna Okaro, who would so often tell me to rest my eyes and take a brake and go to sleep. And to her husband, Michael Okaro, who come in at midnight from work and wake me up with pen in hand and on the paper.

Another special thanks to my sister Ruth Polk and her husband Dewey Polk. Ruth, who furnish a lot of information about our famley and herself and also was my worse critic about what I was writing. Many a night she would turn the light out and tuck me in and the next day she would tell me I need to take a few days off and rest. She would tell her husband Dewey to take me fishing for a few days so I could get my mind off writing so much and relax a while. Yet she was very incouraging and supporting in my writing. Thanks sis.

To my artist who did a grate job drawing and sketching while I try to tell the story, and the hard time she had with me giving instruction on how and what used to be. Thank you Burnice Breckenridge. And to her husband Mr. Breckenridge for his support in incouraging me and his wife whose pictures helped tell the story.

It would not be fair to leave out Frances Wells intire famley for the encouragement they gave me to keep writing. They stood by their mother while she pull together and edit my manuscript with tired fingers and strained eyes and long, long hours. She never grumble, but in her silence, while reading what I had wrote, would at times brake out in a chuckle and a laugh. This would happen when she read one of the funny parts such as "You had to watch my sister Bessie Lee like a hawk watching a chicken."

To all of my supporters, I thank you. And I would like to offer my apologies to those I may have missed.

Eddie Stimpson, Jr., "Sarge"

Introduction

On September 28, 1929, in Collin County, ten miles from Plano, Texas, Eddie Stimpson, Jr., weighing fifteen and a half pounds, was born to Eddie Stimpson (age nineteen) and Millie Stimpson (age fifteen). The young mother, the boy "Junior," and his two sisters all "grew up together," with the daddy sharecropping along a Texas road rich in history and folklore but poor in the luxuries of life.

Preston Road is the oldest north-south road in North Central Texas. On some of the farms along this road, even today, are broken strips of depressed land marking the original route, which ran from the Red River to Austin and San Antonio. This historic route was first used by buffaloes, then by native American Indians. It was a wide path mainly of white rock, old residents have told me. My colleague, the late historian Adelle Rogers Clark, said in 1959:

> No one will ever be able to estimate the number of people who have traveled Preston Road. Many wore moccasins; some were clad in boots; some were swift, some slow. Some came from Europe, others from Canada and Mexico. Many were whites, some were red skinned, others were black. . . .
>
> After the Civil War and the freeing of the Negroes, Kansas offered Negroes inducements to settle there. The Preston was the route of many of these former slaves making their way northward in wagons, on horseback, and on foot.[1]

Some African-Americans and their descendants stayed in Texas; others left but soon returned, riding out the rough years of Reconstruction, of the turn-of-the-century years, of the Depression, of the 1950s. Today, Stimpson muses in his unique spelling style:

> Would any one or any body be interested in what really happen to black famleys during the 1930s when the depression and dust boles? I thought my grand and grate grand kids might read a history book some day and would like to no what happen and how we made it through the 30s out on a farm ten miles north of Plano along Preston Road in Collin County.

The interesting traffic up and down Preston Road apparently never ceased. On pages 149–51, Stimpson tells a believable story of the time Bonnie and Clyde stayed overnight at his folks' house. The outlaws were generous and likable white folks, he says, as he paints a word picture with overtones of the old Robin Hood tales.

When discussing his life as a farmer before and after his twenty-year hitch in the U. S. Army, Stimpson (nicknamed "Sarge") draws on traditional black folklore when he uses a variant of an old tale that says returning to sharecropping has too many "ups" in it. If he had to, Stimpson says he could

> Get up
> Wash up
> Eat up
> Run up the horses
> Feed up
> Catch up the horses

Harness up the horses
Hook up to the plow or wagon
And then you say, Geddie up
After that you may have to pick up rocks
Pull up the corn
Fill up the wagon
And empty up
Put up the horses
Go up to the house
Wash up
Eat up
And go up to bed.

A widely quoted version recorded in the 1950s by black folklorist J. Mason Brewer of Texas appeared in a national anthology in 1957:

> Well, when Ah goes to bed at night, de first thing in de mawnin' Ah got to wake UP; then Ah got to git UP; then Ah got to dress UP—go to the lot an' feed UP. Ah can't let de Mule stan' dere so Ah haf to say git UP; time Ah done work all de summer an' gather UP ma crop an' sell it here Ah come to you to settle UP; you gits yo' pencil out an' figger UP an' say to me, 'Ah'm sorry but you done eat it UP.' Naw, suh, Ah don't think Ah'll try it.[2]

"Tough time never last, but tough people all way do" may be the best single explicit theme of Eddie Stimpson's book. He uses poetry to illustrate his point:

Tough time never last.
Life is sweet. Life is swell.
You can look up. You can look down.
Still, there is nothin to be found.
You can look left. You can look right.
And thing seems out of site.
We no that tomorrow is not promis.
But we don't have to live in sorror.
Don't look back because you won't fine any tracks.
Look ahead. You ain't dead.

Changing from verse to poetic prose is traditional in the black folk speech I have collected in East Texas. At his most original, Stimpson describes the feeling of a young black sharecropper in church on Sunday:

Being young, it was hard to no why I and the other kids would find ourself clapping our hand, patting our feet, and even crying. As I grew older I under stood why. I can remember thing like this: Some one would say, I've sweat all the week in that field for that white man. Now I'm going to enjoy God Day. After sweating all week and blister in hand and feet, this one day I'm free to sing. I can clap my hand because I happy. I can stomp my feet because I glad. I can shout because I feel alive and don't have to worrie bout no body stopping me. This let all the last week burden out. I don't have to think about famley problum. I don't have to worrie bout that bad field of cotton. And I don't have to worrie bout no body telling me what to do.

Stimpson's story grows better and better as you read along and get used to the style and vocabulary. "No" is used for "know," "nabor" for "neighbor," "whin" for "when," and so on. Interestingly, he uses "show" for "sure" (which is usually written "sho'" in black dialect and "shore" in white dialect), but only when "quoting" what he remembers other people saying. He ordinarily spells a word like it sounds to him, although some very difficult words will be spelled correctly. Most interesting are the unusual phrases— like "new ground," understood as "newly cleared land" by rural folk to the third generation. After a day of washing and "wrinching" [rinsing] clothes, you washed your hands with lye soap, sat in a "cain bottom chair," ate by a "karseen" lamp, and stayed away from the "volchars" [buzzards] by staying alive. There is sometimes a serious reflection, such as the startling effect pesticides had on the wildlife in his fields and in his garden, the old-time food supply.

In a lecture at East Texas State University, J. Mason Brewer quoted black folklorist Zora Neale Hurston's recipe for a medicinal tea made of cow chips or sheep droppings. "Why don't you try cow chip tea?" is still heard today in East Texas among the sick. The folk remedies in this book reflect the people's efforts to "do something!" Smutt (soot) from the fireplace, as Stimpson records, really did stop the flow of blood.

Some of the folk customs Stimpson records were, as far as I can tell, largely limited to black families, such as the practice of papering the walls of the house with all kinds of scrap paper to keep out the wind. He writes: "We mix flower [flour] and water for pasting paper. News paper, brown paper sack, Sears catalog." Many of the other black folk customs recorded by Stimpson are similar to those used by poor whites in my own childhood. People swept their bare yards clean with homemade brush brooms (daily in the back yard, if you had chickens) and picked up rocks to put around flower beds. "Mother all way had flowers and mint next to porch." In summer, tubs of water and burlap bags (what Stimpson calls "grass sacks") were kept handy for grass fires in the field. The "straw mattresses" which he refers to seem strange in the land of cotton he lived in, but I have no reason to doubt he slept on them.

"If that don't take the rag clean off the bush" is a mysterious folk saying recorded by black folklorists. Stimpson may explain the meaning in his account of a large white rag always being carried to work by the field hands for the purpose of waving it from hill to hill as a distress signal to call someone at the house.

Many of Stimpson's sketches are full of humor, such as his description of the children getting into the "home brew," but he knows which rituals to take seriously, such as his discussion of how religion helped people keep going or how hog killing time should be cold, but not "blue norther" weather. Stimpson writes "If you ever look to the North and see red over blue, head for cover." Blue is cold wind, red is West Texas sand. "You ain't never been whipped until you get a sand whipping," he says, but Stimpson adds an optimistic note about northers: the blowing sand improved the sticky blacklands around Plano.

Like folk poet J. Mason Brewer, Stimpson uses the dialect speech of his parents and grandparents, although Stimpson's dialect is less exaggerated. Brewer, at East Texas State University from 1969 to his death in 1975, often delighted his folklore students by making up a folk verse for students when a "norther" struck Commerce. Here is an example:

Hyeah dat win' uh whistlin'?
See dem tree limbs shake?
Hyeah dem leaves uh rustlin'?
Hyeah de noise dey make?

See dem geese uh flyin'
To'ds de gulf ergin?
See dem dark clouds sailin'?
Lissen at dat win'!
Dat's uh Norther.

. . . .

Go and git dat kivver
Unnerneaf de bed.
Is you thoo wid supper?
Is de mules all fed?
Bring dat ol' sack tuh me,
Lemme stop dis crack:
Feels uh pain uh runnin
Up an' down mah back.
Dat's uh Norther.[3]

Stimpson's recollections include the recreational activities and "sins" of the Depression era around North Central Texas. His discussions of folk games show the fun of farm life and of Juneteenth holidays. Tap dancing, and even a form of "brake dancing" were common on the Preston Road, as were "the shimmy" and "the chicken." In the shimmy there was a whole lot of shaking going on, and "the chicken" might have been based on chicken fighting, a source of gambling on the Preston Road which frequently led to some violence. There were juke joints, bootleggers (both male and female), and trained dogs chasing rabbits to bet on (with whiskey and women available).

Folk foods aplenty are mentioned early and late. He uses the term "dry salt" to describe pork cured in a barrel with a large amount of salt, including hog jowl for New Year's black-eyed peas. "Biscus" [biscuits] are more rare than corn bread and hominy. Black birds and field larks can be baked in a pie, but more frequently eaten, he says, was wild rabbit, fried in gravy, and served with pork-seasoned "dry salt beans." If a fish was big enough to bite the hook, it was big enough to eat. Wild tea was made from "tea weed" to go with the tiny crisp fish, eaten bones and all.

"Time were tough for many farm and city people," Stimpson says of the Depression, "but it was peoples like mom and dad that kept a lot of people from getting 'miss meal cramps.' So I don't doubt that some where on that road to glory you might see a sign say":

> Millie and Eddie Diner
> Open around the clock
>
> Menue for today
>
> Breakfast
> Bacon or sausage
> Gravy with homemade biscus
>
> Lunch
> Red bean with fat back
> Corn bread
>
> Dinner
> Black bird dumpling
> Or rabbit stew
> Corn bread.

Country folk, black or white, are shown to be superior to city folk, of course. He does quote a folk saying, "If you white, you right. If you black, git back," but there is generally a very balanced view of white people. The chapter paying homage to Mrs. Frances Wells (who helped Stimpson bring the book to final form and helped him find a publisher) and other white friends is moving and eloquent. *My Remembers* is a book of unspoiled simplicity. Read it and see. "Everybody invited and nobody slighted."

James W. Byrd

East Texas State University

---

[1]Adelle Rogers Clark, *Lebanon on the Preston*, (Wolfe City, Texas: Hennington Publishing Company, 1959), 19.

[2]B. A. Botkin, *A Treasury of American Anecdotes*, (New York: Random House, 1957), 47-48.

[3]J. Mason Brewer, *Negrito: Negro Dialect Poems of the Southwest*, (San Antonio: Naylor Printing Company, 1933), 35-36.

Letter to my grands and your grands and there grands:

As you read this book, some of you may think it is not fair or rewarding to print such thing in this day and time. Especial when you look at what some minorities have been through. But remember in my case, in the area I spent my growing up days, it was before black children had the oppitunity to finish high school. My parent and relative, who were raise in the country, had not much chance to go to school and if they did, the fifth grade were as far as they went. English were not that important, and you might be fifteen or sixteen year old when you finish fifth grade. Work in the fields were more important than school. It was matter of survival and support of the famley, so word like "dis" and "dat" or "show" was common word.

You should see the book I learn from. It were ragged with page missing. My mother and

1

father had to learn every thing out of one book. Two at most. Reading, math, and spelling was all they learn. This one of the reason I wrote this book, as reminder to those who can appreciate the advancement made. Not that we want to go back or look back. Remember Lot wife look back and turn to a pillow of Salt, Genesis 19:16.

How do you know where or how far you come if you don't know where you been? I wrote what I know and quote what the old men and women said and how they talk. Thank God they understand each other back then to get us where we are today. We did not get this far by our selfs. Some body did not know how to read or write, but they pray to God and He heard ther prays and had mercy.

2 Timothy 2:14–15 tell us to remember and study for your own self and your own good. It tell us don't cut corners with the truth. It all way bad when you get money in your pocket to think that you come from the other side of the world when you only come from the other side of town.

I think it would be a good story to tell if I could answer the questions I have been asked about my grand parents and ther grand parents. But I don't have much of an answer. As a boy growing up I asked my mother and in later years asked my dad and they could not tell me much. So I thought some day you kids might want to no about your folk and the folk that I grew up with and where and how we made it in my growing up days.

So this is my letter to my grands and your grands and ther grands. Be you black or white, yellow or red, you may have wealth, good health and education, but one thing for sure, you did not get this far in this world by your self. I want you to remember that time was not all way good. Kid hardly ever got past the seventh grade especial the black and the poor white kids. We had to learn early how to work for a living and by the time we got to the age of twelve to fourteen, we had to be able to take charge and care for our famley.

I am going to tell you a little about my life from boy to manhood. And then I am going to tell you some of my remembers, the stories about what was that came tumbling back in my mind. Time were not all way good. I want all of you and your grands to remember that the God that kept us going in the heat of the day through bad time and good time is the same God that keeps you going in your day and time. Remember boys and girls, especial you older boys, that you and I have seen some real bad time together. But the Lord knows and you boys know that I'm very proud of you. I hope and pray and you do the same, that thing will continue to be as good as they are. The best thing for you kid is to get an education. There is no more horse and mule days. There is no more chopping cotton. Education is the key to success. Remember to be obedient to your parents. Go to church and give God the glory. Remember who you are and where you come from.

Don't forget I love you and as long as I live I'm here if you need me. To Frances grand kids and ther grands, remember the heritage of your grand parent and I love you as much as I do my own. To all who read this teach your children something about your growing up days.

Love all way

Eddie Stimpson "Sarge"

My Growing Up Days

The best part of my life were my growing up days. I was born in 1929 in Collin County, Texas, in northwest Plano. If you look north of Spring Creek Parkway before the red light at Preston Road, there is some shade trees there. This is where I were raise from a boy of three year until fifteen year old.

There have been a lot of beautiful land mark destroy in Plano with many of good story behind them. This is one of the reason I pass by my birth place and where I were raise so I won't forget where I come from and how I got this far.

My parents, Eddie and Millie Stimpson, taught me the way of life. My mom taught me how to live. My father taught me how to work and survive, and by the grace of God I've live and survive three wars and a cruel world or you may say cruel problum of this world. God have gave me sixty-two and half years, and I've learned to love all and have patient. I went from a little house to a big house to no house. No matter what, whin or where or how, I'm still very proud to be the country farm boy of Collin County.

During my young year I was all way an out door person—a lover of the natural thing of the world. I suppose it begin back as far as I can remember whin about three years old, born to a fifteen-year-old mother and a nineteen-year-old father with a birth weight of fifteen and a half pound—yugley, meaning ugly and healthy. Being raise in the country, at three I remember out in the pasture running cows through tall weed. Whin my mother would be looking for me and calling, Junior, Junior, and in the evening whin Dad would come home from work and Mother would tell him about me out in the pasture chasing cows and he would get upset.

About that time along came my sister and I was getting in

the way of the midwife known as the baby doctor, a small chershable lady name Mrs. Moody whom I had great respect for all of my young days and still do. I wish I could count the babies she brought into this world.

My mother being a young woman, we grew up together as mother, son, and two sister—four children creating games to play and have fun being a share crop family. There were never no money but plenty of food even if it was gravy and bread. Garden harvest were all way coming and in winter hog killing time. Rag ball with stick bat, mud ball fight, fishing, and walking through the wood was summer time fun.

In winter time checkers, cards, dominoes, snow ball fights, and cardborde sleds. In spite of pulling out all the clothes in winter to cover up with and stuffing walls with rags and paper, I was lying in bed with snow or rain dropping on my face or looking out through the top and counting stars or looking at man in the moon. Growing up in a close nitted family with God and love in our home.

It was a beautiful early age life with a father who was a good provider and a mother with love and understanding. A boy full of energy and all way into some devilish thing. A sister Ruth who were sly and slick with her doing and could con Mother and Dad into beleave anything. And a baby sister Bessie Lee who were as tough as boot leather and thought she could do any thing—a typical tom boy. Bessie Lee and me would create trouble. We would take dry cotton-leave, crumble it up and take any kind of paper and roll the crumble cotton-leave into a cigerett and smoke it. We also would take grape vine sticks and smoke them like a cigar. The stem of the vine did have fine air holes in them. We stole my Dad Prince Albert tobacco until he told me if we were going to smoke we had to buy it. That broke us up. Along with the whipping my mother gave us.

My sister Bessie Lee was a tomboy and would do any thing to stear up trouble and had to be watch like a chicken watch a hawk. She would have to be made to work, even made to do her home work. She would hide whin there were something to do or play sick. Any time we went any where visiting, by the time we got ready to go home, she was all way lost, off playing, or getting into trouble. She got pregnant at sixteen and married, had two boys, got a devorse and married again and had two girls. She is now living in Brownwood and is a evangelist.

Ruth were different from us all. She was the type that would watch us get in trouble and tell mother what we were doing. Ruth did this because she was like a little mother with Bessie Lee and she would do thing with us but would all way try to protect us. She was quite pretty and a book worm. At the age of seven she was smart enough to go to the fourth or fifth grade so they stop her from going to school. The doctor said she was so smart it was effecting her brain. Whin she was about eleven Mother let her go to Dallas to stay with our grandmother and go to a private school. She came back to Plano whin she was in the eleventh grade but got pregnant and did not finish school, but she was well educated. From then on she did what God intended for woman to do: replenish the earth. She had nine kid. She now live in Edgewood, have thirty-two grandkids.

I was the stubborn one and independent. I did what I wanted to even if I got a whipping. Because I lost so much time working to support the family, I was two year in the fifth grade and two year in the seventh. But I did finish high school and taken some college course. I didn't mind working for money. I got out of picking and chopping cotton early in life. By the time I was ten I was driving horse and mules, even car, truck, and tractor. I never will forget at eleven or twelve I drove Ray Haggard Model A truck to Mt. Pleasant to pick up cotton pickers.

All my life I felt that I have been very dependable. I was station in Camp Leroy Johnson in New Orleans. During the three years stay there I meet a girl name Lillie May and married her. We had one child whose name was Wanda Jean Stimpson. This marriage lasted about three and a half years. We were devorse. After this devorse I began to correspond with my high school sweetheart of Plano, Texas. Her name was Willie Ray Kemp. I was still in the Army and in July 1956 we were married and we then had two children, a boy Ivory Tyrone Stimpson and Donna Michell Stimpson. My wife never did travel with me.

Whin Ivory turn twelve and Donna was ten and a half I was going into my twenty-one years of Army life. My wife Willie Ray told me it was time for me to come home and finish help raising my children. On July 30, 1969, I came home to my famley. This marriage lasted thirty-five years until my wife died in 1990.

My mother Millie, a self taught woman, married at thirteen and had her first child at fifteen, me. She was easy going, very humble, grew up with us three kids. She never drink or curse. She kind of live by the book. She would read the Bible, paper backs, hard backs, funny books, Sears Catalogues, anything she could get her hands on. A hard worker and like a mother hen to her kid. She made sure we went to Sunday School and church, even the few times she was not able to go. She read the Bible to us and made us pray every night, and made us work right along with her, what ever it was, in the field or at home. She raise Ruth first child, her first grandchild. She put up with my Dad until we kid were all grown and got a devorse after that. She move to Dallas. She work very hard all her life. She was sickly for a long time, but keep working and raising grand kids. She died in 1964 at fifty-five.

I suppose us kids had our worse time whin Mother had to go to the hospital in Dallas. She was pregnant with a boy. It died because she had malarial fever. She was gone for a month. We got to go see her one time. My dad did not take time to take us. We had to move to Plano and stay with Grandmother. She was good to us, but it was crowded with about six grandkid, four grown up in one little house, three bedroom. There were never enough food. We had plenty food at home, but Dad would not bring any to us. We had plenty chicken, egg, can good at home, but Dad only brought some chicken once. My Mother gave him Hell for it to.

There were several women grew up with my mother. They all care for each other children. There were one lady whom I respected and still do today, Mrs. L. V. Prope. I seen her very often from birth to three or four years. Also my popsye, Mr. Standberry, who I adopted as my second father.

Here are some of the up and down, good and bad, the beautiful and ugly. One of the good things about growing up was the location, a place about ten miles west of Plano, Texas along Preston Road. I knowed every hole where I could go and pull out a rabbit and every tree hollow where I could pull out a possum in a stretch about seven mile long and about three mile wide—never no farther from school than one quarter mile.

There were plenty of woods to hunt small game bird and find wood. There were fishing stream and fishing hole all around and live spring for cool water in the summer. Mother would make tea or lemonade whin there were lemon and sugar. If no sugar it was all way syrup. Any way Mother would fill up jar or jug and put them in the well or in the spring to keep cold for dinner and supper. The ice man would come about twice a week. Until we were able to afford ice box, we would wrap the ice in news paper and grass sack and the ice would last three or four days. There were one other way to keep ice and that were to dig a hole in the ground. We cook on a four hole wood cook stove and a big oven. We stay warm with a shot gun wood stove.

In the winter month whin Dad and the other nabor were not out hunting or cutting wood, we would sit around the fire and pop horse corn, which is yellow dent corn. While shucking and shelling corn, Dad would pick out the large grain, put them in a seprate container to make hominy. Dad would set up a board about a four foot by four foot, which was mostly a tailgate from out of a wagon, prop it up out in the yard, put corn under it, and run a long wire from the prop to the door of the house where we could peep out. Whin the bird, black bird or field lark, would feed under the tailgate, he would pull the prop and trap the bird and wait a few minutes for the bird to die, then go and collect the bird. Whin we had enough we would pluck and clean them. Mother would fry and make dumpling and corn bread. These birds were means of having a meal on the table. There were all way meat from the hog killing: fat back, sausage, and ham and dry salt (bacon that had been salted down).

Like I said before there were all way plenty of food, but to get out and kill rabbit, squirrell, bird, it was fun, plus they were good food with gravy and biscus and gravy and corn bread. It was all way the same thing year round. In the spring there were fish added to the menu. In the summer there were bean, potatoes, rice, fat back, corn bread, and biscus every day of the week. On Sunday chickin fixed every which way. Some type cake with icing or a flavored sugar dip or syrup or molasses. Every once in a while during the summer month we would all get stake or roast. Mother would save eggs, pick out some old hen, and carrie them to town and trade for meat, sugar, flour, and baking needs.

While on the subject of trading food in the city, I guess city life never did really take a hold of me and I still don't care for city life. I'm a farmer and out door life person. I don't care for the four wall or mall. So whin we would get to go to town maby two or three time a year, there were time whin mother and father would go to town and I would rather stay home, go hunting or fishing, watch the animal, birds, look for bug and snakes. Not that I would catch snake, but I would kill them, especial whin my dad learn me how to shoot the .22 rifle and bought me a BB gun—a 300 shot Daise BB gun.

Whin we would go to town I would all way observe how Mother would shop, especial the printed design flour sack. My sister would pick out the color because these were the sack mother would make there clothes from, including there under clothes. Most of the clothes we got were made of hand me down. We got one pair of shoes a year, maby a pair of ducking and flannel shirt. That were for school and church only. Trade day in McKinney was all way a good day to meet and see friend, eat hot tamale sold on the street from a push cart, and bring home some candy. My younger sister were all way good at hussling up some cookies or candy. She would share with us but gobble it up as fast as she got it. Me, I would take my time eating and Ruth would save hers until we had ate ours just to tease us, a day later passing it under our nose and not giving us any.

Ruth were the quiet type, while Bessie Lee and me were cooking up thing to do, making up game to play, catching bug and grass hopper, tying string to there leg, and making kites that would not fly. Mother would make rag ball to play ball with. We all like base ball because Dad was a good base ball player, playing ball at least once or twice a week, Saturday and Sunday. Dad was a pitcher and a good one. He was my ideal. He was good enough to go to the Southern Negro League. He and Shep Hutchang went and play about two month through the South—Lousianna, Mississippi, and Atlanta. I guess he got

I like school very well. I had to go through the fifth grade two year and the seventh grade two year because I had to help support the family.

home sick, for the family and the farming was part of Dad life.

Back to my self. At five year old I was going to the corn and wheat field driving a team of horses and mules. At six I had to chop or pull grass out of our cotton. At seven I was cooking dinner for the famley. I had learn to cook dry salt beans and corn bread. I never have forgot whin mother and Dad came home one evening and I had cook supper. Whin they taste the bean and corn bread, it was different. I had put oinion and tomatoes in the beans and used bacon grease in the corn bread. From then on Mother wanted me to cook the bread. I never did learn how to make biscus or make cake, and I still don't bake cake or fool with dough. I do a lot of cooking these days. I like to experiment on thing.

I like school very well. I had to go through the fifth grade two year and the seventh grade two year because I had to help support the family. I think the excitement with me was school—the starting and stopping for cotton picking and back to school to be with friend who for several month I had not seen, except on some Saturday whin the farm kids would meet up in town.

I were never very good in math. But I could read and add good so I taken on the job of keeping cotton weight, also figuring out the pay each day of those who want to get paid. Ray Haggard would check that day to see how many wanted to get paid. At quitting time here would come Mr. Ray with a sack of money. I had also learn how many pounds it took to make a bale of cotton. You wanted to have at least a full bale or full two bales whin you hauled it to the gin.

I did graduate from high school in Plano Colored High under the professorship of Turner in 1948. That same year I went into the Army. I shall never forget the day I went to McKinney and join the Army. Glenn Kemp went with me because he and I were the only boys graduate that year—five girls and two boys. So he and I decided to go into the service.

But before we go on let me stop and inject the story of the greatest woman whom I admired so much, my grandmother Corrie, my dad mother. She were six foot and over weight—three something—solid built and a masterful fisher woman. She love to fish and would all way catch fish. From the time that I could remember, grandmother would come to the country and stay two or three day at a time, so Dad would drive her to Lake Dallas or the Frisco Lake or Dr. Dye creek which were White Rock Creek. That were where all the picnicks and baptisement were held. My Dad were not a fisher man. But my mother, grandmother, and I were. Until I learn how to drive, which were at seven or eight, Dad would take us to the lake,

Corrie Drake Stimpson

leave us, and come back and get us. Whin we got home grand-mother would start cleaning fish and mother would start frying them no matter how late it were. One thing, it did not matter how big or how small the fish grandmother catch, she brought it home. If it were big enough to bite, it were big enough to eat. As I got older whin Dad would turn me loose with the car, I would go get grandmother and we would go fishing somewhere, she and I and another lady name Monk, her fishing partner. We would sit on the creek, hot or cold, and fish. I've seen time it would be raining and freezing. Whin we got froze out, we would leave and go by the liquor store and pick up her a pint of whiskey and she would sip on it for weeks at a time. She just liked to have a little nip for the cold. After I went into the service I would come home on leave and all we did were go fishing, some time stay all night. I were in Germany whin she died, and my aunt told me the last thing she said was whin was I coming home to take her fishing.

One of the thing that I love about my grandmother, she were very out spoken, say what were on her mind and very protective over her family, especial the children. She keep up with all the news. Anything anyone wanted to no, go to the corner of what now 13th Street and H Street, and get the latest news from my grandmother.

I had the oppitunity to live in her home whin my mother were in the hospital in the late thirties or early forties. Time were very hard—no money, very little food in town, no fire wood. We would walk the rail road track and pick up cole. In the winter month I think the white train men would throw it off or open the trap doors a crack whin checking the wheel bearing. They would do this between the R.R. trestle which crosses Spring Creek south of present Plano Parkway and where the tracks cross Highway 5. Some body would be watching and run the mile and a half to Colored Town, down the trail through the woods, on past the slaughter house and J. W. Shepherd mule pasture, and bring word that the cole train was coming or just went by. Whin that message come they grab them a bucket or two and head for the tracks. Before you know it the track were pick clean and people would say, Those train people sure were good to us today.

My dad would bring can food and chickin from the country once a week to help feed us three kids along with four or five more kid. Through it all with the help of God we made it. The war came along and thing got better. My dad were call, but being a farmer, he did not have to go. The boss would all way go to the draft board to sign a deferment.

With the war going on thing began. Peoples become more drawing together. There were more concern about one another. White and black began to speak with each other with a little more love because son and husband and father were call away. Prayers were more often in home. The jobs increase. There were more money coming in. The black were still held out of good position or job, but pay were better and respect were better. Predjudice still exist but with more respect. During this time I were in my teens and for the first time I was invited into a white family home and set down at there table and ate. I got full, but the food was much different taste—no season or taste.

As a teen I were able to get a job. While on the subject of jobs I can remember the first job I made money and that was clearing up wooded bottom. We would clear out dead trees, cut it into cord or ricks, hall it in wagon to Plano, and sell the wood seventy-five cent a cord. My next job were building fence to coral cow and horses, making about seventy-five cent a hour for a rich doctor out of Dallas. The cheapest work were chopping cotton, doing the same work that the grown up were doing, but my pay were a half a hand. Full pay were $1.25 an hour. My pay were sixty and a half cent an hour.

My next job were with the Wells Brothers whin I was about thirteen working as a block and tie with a stationary hay bailer, seventy-five cent a hour from the hay field to corn sheller, sacking corn. I would gather scrap iron in my spare time. All summer my dad and uncle would hall it to Dallas.

My dad all way had want farm work—strictly a farm boy. Between 1910 and 1920 a number of black famleys began to split up and move to Plano. Some could afford to buy a lot and house, some just buy lots and build shack on them. This was after they get there crop. My dad would not move to town so an uncle taken him in. That were in between 1915 and 1918. Any way in 1918 at the age of twelve he raise his first crop of cotton. He had share cropped twelve acre for Ray Haggard. Out of his share of the crop he taken $180 and had a roof put on his mother house in Plano. Dad stay with Ray Haggard as share cropper and field hand and finely rear his famley on those twelve acre until we move to Allen farm in 1944. Then we move

15

back to Ray Haggard again, but we move to a smaller house, no more share cropping, work for little or nothing, all most like starting a new life all over.

After a cuple of year we move to Vera and Si Harrington place where Uncle Grady and Jim Haggard use to live. Quentin Robinson had taken over leasing the Harrington farm. Dad was working in town. Mother was finding house work in town and I was working on the farm. We stay there a cuple of years, then move over to Fred Harrington place where my mother and I would wash and iron for house rent. Of course I was still doing farm work for Quentin Robinson and Fred Harrington. I finely at fifteen landed a good job with Mrs. Ammie Wilson, who paid good and a steady job. With my mother finding work in town and me working, Mother and my two sister had it pretty good. Dad had left us but that another story.

No one beleave I were going into service. I were in high school whin the recruting officer came to my house and talk to me about service. He put me on his list and said for me to finish my schooling first and he would get back to me. My cousin A. C. Stimpson and his wife Genevah came to me and told me they would put me through college if I wanted to go. Being pretty smart in high school, also a good football player, base ball pitcher, and basket ball player, it would get me into college. But I was very independent type person. I wanted to make it on my own. So I finish school in May and on July 9, 1948 went to McKinney and join the army. I were very much in love with Willie Ray Kemp and for her I did not want to leave. But she did not want to get married at that time and I left for service and made a career—twenty-one years, and this is another part of my life.

Changes on the Farm

As we continue life day in and day out, night after night the years creep by us before we even realize where they have gone. So as you read, let your mind drift back to the thirties and forties, and I will attempt to guide you through one of the most dramatic changes of the times and how effective it was as it touched the life of the farm famleys. Famleys were being seperated by the Depression and then after the prosperous period that followed, were seperated again by the war. This time young man and fathers left for city jobs or were called to war. Those left behind had to double and triple there work load. It was once sun up to sun down. We soon found ourself working some time twelve to fifteen hour a day, which took us into the night especial during harvest.

As a boy growing up there were two different kinds of life involved in this story of my boyhood. As a black boy who run bare foot all summer and hole in shoes in winter, I came in contact with the men who were the big land owners and I realize they were an asset to the poor white or black famley who had no land nor a house to live in. You had three choices. You could move on a land owners farm who would let you share crop or you could work for him by the day. Or you could do like many black and whites did and that was to live like gypsies, hall your famley and everything you own, on to a team of mule and cover wagon or a old car or truck, pitching tent along the road side over night, and stopping by every body house and every land owner, picking up little odd job be it chopping cotton, picking cotton, or clearing bottom land for firewood. I seen all of this.

My father was a share cropper until he left Haggard place to try to make it as a tenant on Lavon Farm. I really don't no if there were any other black share cropper farmers in and

17

around during my growing up days other than my dad and Bud Thorton on the Harrington place. Being a share cropper famley we were able to live better than the field hands.

As a share cropper son during the Depression and dust storm days, I saw the life of many farm owners as well as black farm hand famleys changed. I remember by the time the Depression was over the only one that was left on the farms was the older man and woman and young children. Those in the age from around fourteen or fifteen years to those in there twentys disappeared. This was one of those time we would see lot of travel coming by my house. I remember some saying they were going to California. Some say Chicago and some to New York. I remember those that were in school, the older ones, would disappear.

Although farming were about the safest place to keep you from going hungry, there were no money and no crop to work. The drought had burn up the crop. It had dried up creek and shallow wells along creek beds. During this time the only ones left on the farm had access to water. I can remember well that we had a live spring. We dug it out enough to hold water. So we carried water to the garden in order to raise food. People who had no access to water had to move on somewhere else.

I also remember during this time a lot of men coming through the country promise to find water on the farms. Oil digger came and dug well on the owner farm for a little or nothing, any where from $25 to $100. I think those who could find water charge about $25. Some time the farm hand and nabors farm hand team up to dig the well.

Because of the drought, white farmer son and daughter as well as white and black share cropper who had son and daughter fourteen or fifteen or older left and move into the city, move with other famley or made it on there own in other part of the United State. During that time it was nothing for two or three famley to move into one house together in the city, sometime building another patch up room on to the all ready run down house.

In the late thirties the dust storms gone, the earth around Collin was rich and the crop was florshing. Cotton, corn and wheat was making good and the market was good. Crowded famleys in town began to thin out as the old farm houses that had been empty for several years came to life again with middle age farmer or farm hands. In Collin County most of the blacks come in from South and East Texas. The white farmers and farm hands come from Oklahoma and Kansas. The crops were good enough for this part of Texas to draw people from far and near. Although many farmers were still mostly using horses and mule, larger owners were able to buy a tractor along with hiring more help. The dust bowl had come and gone along with the Depression, and the economy was just about to stabilize itself. Over all thing began to look good for farming famleys.

So here it was. We crawl into the thirties, we almost faded away during the mid thirties, we came to a bright and blooming late thirties, a smooth ride into the early forties with smiles and happiness. Then all of a sudden we woke up one day in 1941 and the dream we had began to slip away. And blooming as farming was, and bad as the world needed its commodities, the farmers found out that we were all most as bad off as what we had just came through. It was Mother Nature taken its toll in the thirties. Now in the forties human nature began to take its toll.

The war came. Those able to work was ship off to war. That left old men, women and children to work the farm. There were a few middle age men that got deferment from service. But as the war pick up, factory in city opened. This draw the middle age men, young and old women to the city looking for a better living. Of course the money was better, but it left very few farm hand to work the crops which was badly needed to feed people. But as it was thing got worse. Even the farm peoples had to rely on commodities from the relief county agent. Horse and mules began to disappear. They were use for food and army use. So for a half decade farming suffered another set back. It was quite a struggle. Crop were plentiful but labor were few. Every one no time was about to make another change. Materialistic things changed. New inventions of equipment take the places of old.

A few years ago before my dad died, he and I would ride through the country together and talk about how it use to be and what ever happen to certain houses, barn and old tractors. There are only a few old timers who still think about old times. But I think you grand and great grand children, no matter who you are, need to no about how folks made it during those Depression and dust bowl years. This is my story as I remember what happen and how it happen in those faded years rolled by.

Famley Problum

All that have been said and did, what I have talk about was the good and some bad about my family living on the farm.

Thing did not go to well with Mom and Dad. He was a man that like women. And I think it was from the Stimpson genes. It has been said that the Stimpsons were highly sexually attractive. Only those who are knows. All of the thing Dad did, he was still a very good provider, he work six and a half and seven day a week. He was not book educated, but he sure did no the farming and all way made good crops.

Also, out of all the arguing Dad and Mom had, he never raise his hand to hit her—even the time she and I walk five miles leaving Bessie Lee and Ruth home. We went to the house where Dad was visiting a woman. We peep in the window. The woman was sitting in Dad lap. Mom kick the door down. The woman ran out the back door and Dad got up and stroll on out to the car, Mother and I behind him. Whin we got back home Mom jump out of the car, run into the house, got the shot gun and as Dad come in the door she raise the gun to shoot him, and Ruth and Bessie Lee standing beside her jump and swung down on the barrel. Without Ruth and Bessie Lee, Dad would have been shot gun dead, but all the shots went into the floor. After that Dad was a good boy for years.

I guess we were grown whin she got after him again and she caught him again at a woman house and call him out and chaise him down the street with a pen knife. She did not catch him. The knife was to small to put a scratch on him any way. After that she gave up on Dad. They soon got a divorse. We were all grown and had left home. I went to the Army and sent money to her every month until she died. Ruth move to East Texas, Bessie Lee move to Garland. Dad married again, work with the Carpenter Ford House, then back to the farm. After he

Whin we got back home Mom jump out of the car, run into the house,
got the shot gun and as Dad come in the door she raise
the gun to shoot him.

retired he went into the mowing business for a few years. Then
he quit work at about seventy-five year old and died at eighty-
one in 1988. He use to say all the time that if he ever got sick
he guess he would die. He did. All of his life he was never sick,
except every once in a while he would have chill.

I have no regret of what hard time we had. Without the
hard time I could not appreciate the good time in this world. It
is not all way the way you want it. But thank God for giving
you the sense to accept the good, the bad, and the ugly. It up to
the individule to choose the one they would like to be.

A Vision of What Was

The following is some thing that has been ask, just to jot my remember. By the research and question Ive ask, it help me to fill the remember that I had forgot, but if ask I can remember. As I write, in the back of my mind I ponder the thing I remember before I paint a pitchure, then put it on paper just the way I hear and see it. I don't write what I can't see or hear. From my remember I would like for who ever read or look at the pitcher to concentrate and visionalize as if you were there and I were narration you through my life, and the surrounding I grew up in.

The first house I live in that I can remember were whin I were about three. It were a shot gun house, tin top, located east of Preston Road near the creek bed. I remember because soon as we move there were a bunch of cows in the pasture and the weeds were high as I was. Mother miss me and she was standing on the small porch calling me. She said she seen the cow running and my head bouncing up and down. Whin I got to the little house of two room she chewed me out.

There were a kitchin and a big room. The kitchin were so small Mother say she could not hardly turn around. We eat and sleep in the same room. In the kitchin were a wood four burner stove and cabnet for flour and potatoes. There were shelf all around for dishes and can food. Silver ware were kept in a gallon bucket. Pot and pan were kept on and in the cookstove. There were one window. The stove pipe went out the back of the house, not the top.

The big room had a iron bed and a cot. Dad and mom slept in the big bed. I slept on the cot. All the furniture we had were a homemade table and big dresser with four long drawers and a small stand beside the bed for the oil burner lamp and a can for Dad cigerette. A tin wood burner stove for heat with the stove pipe out the top. About three cain bottom chairs and a stool. There were clothes rack in one corner close to the front door. There were a window on both side of the house and one door in front. Only one door in the house, that the front door. A small porch, no stairs.

This is the house Ruth were born in. I don't remember too much about her birth. We live there about two or three years. Then we move up to the big house.

I think whin Mom got word we could move she carried all she could by hand that day with Ruth and me tottling along with her, each trip probly with a little bag or bucket helping out. I don't remember where we got furniture from, but Dad would come in with bed and chairs. Every once in a while Mother would tell Dad whin he got in, Lets go over to see Mrs. Clough or Aunt Emma or Mrs. Charity. Some one would have done give us something. I remember we went to Forney, Texas, one Sunday evening to get some furniture from my grandmother, Moms mother.

Mother were so proud. She scrub the floor, paper the house all over. It was like the beginning of a new life for her. She were happy about all the room she had. She let out a sound, Wow, a Home at last!

I remember after we finish papering the house mom would stand back and look, then say, Let decorate the wall. We mix flower and water for pasting paper. News paper, brown paper sack, Sears catalog. During the year we would all way do some papering of the house but come Xmas season, we went into full swang of papering the house and decorating the wall.

I'm not a artist but back in my mind I can see this second house I live in as a boy and the surrounding where I grew up, the house and barn, hog pen, mule barn and grain barn where me and my sister play in. Can you pitcher a famley living in the country out in the middle of a paster with all the barn, animal, trail, stream, spring. As I write I look at the sketch I drew and look back and try to describe the place I grew up.

As I look at the surrounding I see my two story house. A chicken house, turkey pin, fiting chicken pin my Dad had. A trail to the mail box on Preston Road. A road from the front of the house through the paster to the highway. A trail behind the house to the outdoor toilet. A trail to the well along the stream behind the house. The same trail go across the stream to the horse and mule barn, the grain barn, hog pen and garden.

Now I will attempt to describe the house. A two story house, tin top with hole in the roof. Every time it rain, we start getting the tub and bucket, pot and pan to catch the water, sometime moving the bed around to keep from getting wet. There were four rooms down stair and a big open room up stairs.

The kitchin were a small room with a iron wood stove with four burner, on top a big oven. There were a table for working and prepairing the food, a cabnet or two, a flour cabnet with place for potatoes and oinion. Coming out of the kitchen into a big dinner room where we ate, there were a big table, five cain bottom chairs, some cabnet and a closet where we kept our hog meat once it was salted down for a length of time. The meat, ham, shoulder and bacon were first put in a wood box, salted down and rubbed with salt every two or three days till all the blood drawed out and the meat was cured. Some time this might take about a month, depending on the weather. During warm weather it would cure a lot faster. Once cured the meat was took out and hung beside the sacks of sausage wrapped in cheesecloth—sometimes fifteen, twenty sacks hanging there. The kid were kept out of this closet unless I was cooking and went in to cut a piece of meat to cook with my beans. There were a back door and a porch and a front door to come out on the porch that stretch all the way from the front living room to

A home at last.
The house on
Preston Road.

the end of the kitchin. While we eat, water would be on the stove getting hot for dish washing. We wash and wrinch and dry the dishes on the eating table and place them in a wall cabnet. The kitchin and dishes was clean after each meal.

Whin you leave out of the dinner room you come into my bedroom. This room had the upstairs steps in it. My iron bed queen size, a dresser and a closet under the stair steps. I use to lye in my bed and look through hole in the upstairs and hole in the roof and see stars. We had a lot of rats, big ones. One night I was lying in my bed and look up in the corner of the roof upstairs. I kept seeing sparks flicker. I look and look. It was some thing I had not seen before so I call Dad and told him about it. That brought all the other famley in my room to see what was going on. Dad went upstairs and it was a fire. The rat had made a cotton bed and carried some kitchen matches in its bed and had struck them and started a fire. That taught us what a rat could do. We start to keep our matches in a can or a jar with a top to it. I still do that today. Dad use to shoot them in the house with a BB gun. We finely got two big persian cat. We had no more trouble out of rats. We had to worry about what the cat would bring in the house. Them cat would bring rat, rabbit, bird and finely snakes. After the snake we start locking them outside. So much for cat and rat.

Lets go to the next room which is the largest room in the house. This was call the famley room. There were two bed, for Dad and Mom, and Ruth and Bessie Lee, two dresser, a table, three or four chairs, and a long cast iron wood stove, almost in the middle of the room. Two karseen lamp, one on the table where we kid got our lesson, one where Mother would sit and read her funnies book, paper back book and the Bible. We all had chair to sit in. In the summer month we would sit out on the other front porch. If the mosquitoes was bad we would put rag in tin bucket and make smoke can to keep the mosquitoes away. In winter we sit around the stove till bed time.

Up stairs was a open space mostly kept for storage space. But we did not have to worrie about storage. We didn't have nothing to store any way. We kid play up stairs. And Dad kept his homemade beer up there.

There were plenty of room in the house. No one had to stumble over each other except Bessie Lee. Some one was all way hollering at Bessie Lee to get out from under me. I think the only complaint we had was whin it rain, and whin it was cold Mother would say, I wish Mr. Ray would fix the top. And whin it got cold we start paper the wall and stuffing rag in hole. We take can top and nail over rat hole. We mix flour and water for pasting paper on the wall. News paper, brown paper sack, Sears catalog. Mother would piece quilts and buy cotton roll with cotton picking money. After wheat harvest we would gather wheat straw, take the old cotton sack, sew them together, make a mattras sack, and stuff it with straw to make mattras.

That about it for the living house. Lets go outside and see what all the other building and trail lead to. There were all way horses, mules and cows, some time sheep. So we had a fence around the house. Mother love flowers and all way had flowers and mint next to the front porch and kitchin porch. We had a "swept yard," was kept swept every day. We kids would go out and pull broom weeds. Mother would twist and tie them together and make brooms. Each day Mother and us kids would sweep the yard all around the house, even in back where the chickins were kept. If there was rocks too big to sweep we picked them up and stacked them up to use for edging the flower beds. The yard was so clean no weeds or grass could grow. Whin it was dusty we would hall water and sprinkle the yard down before we swept. During the summer whin the stubble fields were burnt off, sometimes the wind might switch and catch the dry pasters on fire and spread all the way up to the fence which ran all around the house. If we didn't have a clean "swept yard" the house would probly be burned. We kept tubs of water and grass sacks (burlap bags) handy during the summer whin the grass started drying up.

Mother took pride in her yard and flowers like she did her house. On Saturday she would say, We may have company tomorrow so we need to sweep the yard cleaner—today. Mother had tried flowers along the yard fence line but the horses and cows would eat them up so we moved back from the fence and made flower beds in each corner of the yard.

Let see if I can describe the other thing. The road leading from the front of the house went to Preston Road. The house in the back of the big house is the chickin house. At least the chickin stay dry whin it rain. That was one thing we did have plenty of—chickin and turkey. My mother love to raise them. Chickin and turkey money was her money to use as she see fit. If she thought she was not going to get enough setting hens, she would scrape up enough money and go to McKinney and order hen, 50 or 100 for about five or ten dollar.

The trail leading out the back door went to the well and spring and across the creek to the barn. There were a horse and mule barn with feed trough, corn crib, and hay rack. The barn also had a fence around it to hold the working team. The working teams were also harnest up in this lot, and were walk out back to the wagon or plows and hook up for the day work.

The next barn were a grain barn, divided in to three or four room. Corn, wheat, oat, barley, and cotton seed were preserve for feed and planting seeds. This was one of us kid play spot. We would swing from rafter to rafter and drop down in the grain, play like we were Tarzan the Apeman.

The other shed were the hog pen. There were all way plenty of hog. Ray and Daddy kept their hogs there and any body elso who live on the Ray farm. Most of the time I did all the feeding, all way corn.

I forgot the little house out by itself behind the big house. This was the outdoor toilet. I think this complete the area where I live. Oh I forgot the trail to the mail box.

The school and church building was across Preston Road and 500 yards to the west of the road. It was place across the creek there on the Harrington land and called Shepton Colored School and Shepton Church. More about this later.

Famley Life

Famley life during my growing up as a share cropper was not an easy life, and to make things comfortable the famley had to be very close such as knowing one anothers problems. You all sit down and ate together. Each member had their own duties to do and if one had a hard time doing their share, the other famley members would help out. If I chop the wood, my sisters and mother would pick up the chips and help carry the wood in the house. If some one come up with a game, the others would make the game work in a fun way. If we were in the field chopping cotton, if one got a clean row and one got a bad row, you help out. You had prayer together every night. You sit around and told everybody what you did that day. You went to church together every Sunday and prayer meeting on Wednesday night. Mother would read the Bible to us.

We got our school work together. It was good for my mother to help get school work out because of her lack of finishing school. She was in the fifth grade whin she dropped out to get married. And she continued to hang around school whin she could until I was born. She learned schooling with me all the way through high school. Self taught education.

My Dad could not read or write but he was good in math, adding and subtracting and dividing. If math was too hard he would use grain or corn to figger out a problem.

If any one got sick, they stay in bed and the others would wait on you hand and foot. In my famley we did every thing together. My mother being as young as she was, she was like a child herself, so she grew up with us three kids. If one of us said or did anything wrong we got whip. Mother would all way send us kids out to get our own switch. If you came back with one too small, you went and got another one until you got enough to plait together. She would all way whip the back, butt, and legs. She did not believe in using her hands unless it were the spur of the moment. She did not slap or hit you any where around the head.

My dad only whip me two times and that was for telling a lie and putting a snake on my sisters. I thought he had gone to sit down and rest from work, but he was standing at the back door looking. To this day I remember every lick. We as a famley were so close that if one was hurt we all hurt. A famley that prays together stays together.

They gave me the name George Stimpson at birth but changed it to Eddie Jr. They never went back to court to change my name. I remember in later years my mother told me about the naming. I've had a big problum getting my birth certificate.

A midwife by the name of Mrs. Moody birthed Ruth and Bessie Lee. She got out of the Model A car looking so motherly like in her bonnet and long black dress and her black bag.

A midwife by the name of Mrs. Moody birthed Ruth and Bessie Lee. Mrs. Moody lived in Plano and whin the time came someone would drive to town or send a message. She didn't drive but her husband or someone would drive her out and sometimes she had to stay several days till the baby was born. I remember so well whin Dad drove up with her whin my baby sister Bessie Lee was about ready to be born. She got out of the Model A car looking so motherly like in her bonnet and long black dress and her black bag. The black shoes she wore were hightop and laced halfway and hooked halfway. She spent the night and whin the time came, she told my father to get some sheets and rags together, get a fire going in the kitchen stove, and get some water boiling. I was five so she sent me to go to the well and start hauling water, pail after pail. Then whin we finish, she said, All of you get out of here now.

Ruth was named for the Bible from the Book of Ruth. Bessie Lee was named after her Aunt Bessie, Mother's sister. Most of my years, one through six, I wore dresses at home or around the house. There was all way more girl clothes than boy clothes. During all of my growing up days there never seemed to be any boys.

The wonderful things I remember about my famley was doing every thing together, from playing games together out side to playing games inside. Even the fussing and fighting, every body got involved so it would come out so no one had the advantage over the other. All were happy about the situation.

Getting a Wife

One day I got to wondering how my mother and dad come to get married. Of course I no the boys and girls was very much acquainted because they all lived nabor to each other. They got to see each other whin they walk those three to seven mile to school together. In good weather they cut across the fields. In bad weather they went around on the roads.

They had an even better oppitunity to get closer to each other at the parties, especial during those days whin there was a party each week and the famleys would go together from house to house. There was all way sodie pop, ice tea, lemonade and for the grown up folks, beer, wine and whiskey. There was all way food too—bolonie, sandwich, fried chicken, potato salad and plenty cookies and cakes. And music. There was all way music. Uncle Devil Horse, my dad-dad, and grandmother brother, could really play the gitar and banjo. He would play for all the parties in and around the community, both black and white.

At those parties there was all way somebody there or came by to play the gitar or banjo, piano, or just beat on a pan or bucket. Those parties were not only an oppitunity for the boys and girls to get together but men and women who may not no each other might drop by for a good time. There was never no problum knowing whin the party was or where, especial when Uncle Devil Horse were going to be playing.

Kids, unless I share these stories with you, you would never know how much of a part Uncle Devil Horse and my father play in the history of this community. I feel my dad was a great asset to the community and could have been better if the chance or times was right.

Another way the boys got to see the girls was they would drop by the field where the girls would be chopping or picking cotton. The courting some time would get plenty serious in the cotton patch or corn patch. Once the boys and girls could figger out how to get away from there parent, they would say, Dad or Mom, I'm going to the other end and chop or pick my way back.

Whin I ask my mom how or why she marrie dad, she said, My and his famley were picking cotton and Eddie, your father, came through the cotton field one day. He seen me and talk to me and the others. And he was a good look man. He told me he was going to marrie me. He went and ask my father and mother for me and we got married.

Like most men in those days he went directly to the source. That was the mother and father. If they saw a girl they want, they chase until they got her or went to the mother and father. They ask and they got.

My dad did not talk much, but he was a handsome man and he had his own cotton crop. My dad was six when his dad died at an early age and his mother move to town. My dad refuse to move with his famley but moved in with his mother brother, Uncle Ronney. He work the fields follering in the footsteps of his grandparents, Andy Drake and Mose Stimpson. He learn all he could about farm animals, and planting of seed. In other word, dad was a rare type of young man. He learn about how many eggs a chickin layed before she would set and how long it take a stalk of corn to bear a ear of corn to eat. So he must've been doing something pleasing to Ray Haggard because at the age of twelve, he heard Mr. Ray say, Do you think you can handle a crop of cotton?

Yes, Sir.

Well, you are twelve and I am going to give you twelve acres of cotton on halves.

Thank you, Sir. You won't be sorrowful about it.

It stand to reason that dad was looked up to because he become a share cropper at age twelve and then stuck with it.

Whin I ask my mom how or why she marrie dad, she said, My and his famley were picking cotton and he came through the cotton field one day. He told me he was going to marrie me. He went and ask my father and mother for me and we got married.

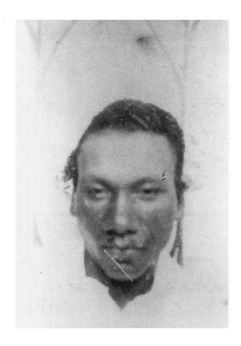

37

He was well known as the only black share cropper, young or old, at that time. The rest was day laborers.

So at nineteen he was a good look man and well thought of by white and black. My mother say, It had been very hot in the cotton field, dragging that sack, and this man came by and I no him because we were all nabors. I was a little shy but I think I was glad. And whin he told me he was going to marrie me, it did both scare me and kinder made me feel good. First thing I thought about, I would be able to leave home like all girl wish. And I would be able to get out of the cotton patch. Well, I was able to leave home, but I never got out of the cotton patch.

At the time dad married my mom there was four girls at her home, Mother being not the oldest but the largest of the four. Dad pick her. Times were hard. There were no money and mom father was glad to get rid of a girl especial to some one who had a job and was a worker.

As I recall the wedding of my Aunt Senie, my mother sister, was on a Sunday morning right after church service. The announcement was made that there's a wedding on this morning. My aunt and my uncle were to walk down the isle together. My grandmother, the bride mother, was seated on the front row. I guess she was there for a reason because my grandmother Birks did not go to church that much. After the preacher, Sister Riddle, finish, the bride and groom walk back down the isle together out the door. There were people line up outside and some type of seeds were thrown at the cuple. It could've been wheat seed or beans, maby a little rice. As they walk to the car some man held the door open. The bride and groom got in, drove off while a bunch of us kids was running behind trying to catch up to the cans tied behind the car, as the cans went banging, jumping and bumping down the little road to highway 289. The cuple drove to her husband famley home as was usual with newly weds. This give strength to the young famley.

Aunt Senie's the only wedding I can recall. But I think it was customary for cuples to get a license. I no my mom and dad had one. And I no this too. Marriages back then had closer ties and last longer.

Come on Kids, Lets Eat!

From about the time I was seven years old I've been cooking. During my early years most of your food were garden raised. Pinto beans, onions, cabbage, carrots, potatoes (Irish and sweet), corn (yellow dent and white), tomatoes, radishes, mustard and turnip greens, asparagus, dill, cucumber, and okra. Water mellon and cantalope was planted along with the cotton. A desenated spot in the field were picked out and the seed was drop in the planter box with the cotton seed. Every thing you raise in the garden were harvest and canned for winter months whin there were no going to town but maybe once a month.

Canning season was very hard work. There were always plenty of plums and wild blackberries, peaches for jelly whin corn were ripe. You pull, shuck, silk, cut off the corn, and can. Whin it was harvest you shuck and shell, pick out the good grain, and made hominy. Shell corn were taken to the mill and grind up for corn meal.

Pinto beans were pick early for green beans, and some time there were fresh Irish potatoes mix with the green beans with a piece of dry salt for season. All the vegetables were canned in fruit jars. Finely my mother were able to get a canner and a pressure cooker and a can sealer. Cabbage were use to make chow chow. Most farming famleys main meals consist of red beans, dry salt or ham bone, potatoes, corn bread, biscus and gravy—breakfast, lunch, and supper. Day in and day out, year round.

There were all way plenty of chickin and eggs. Winter time it was rabbit, squirrel, possum. Birds were fry with dumpling or smother in gravy same as rabbit. Dad could take a jack rabbit and make chili. The hog head was cook whole and have enough meat for a family of five to eat a whole week.

Canning Season was very hard work.

Yellow dent corn were use for pop corn in the cold winter months whin we sat around the wood heater in the bedroom. Okra were cook as is or made gumbo with tomatoes, oinion, garlic, and peppers cook together. Tomatoes were use for preserve. There were time mother would make vegetable soup. She would take all the different can vegetables, put them together, cook it, and then make corn bread. The only thing I never did cook were anything to do with flour dough and still don't. I'm a good cook and can cook anything. I learn most of my cooking from experience, no receipts. I like to do a lot of experimenting, cooking anything as long as it don't have to do with dough.

Other thing for cool dinner drinks were lemonade, wild tea, and vanilla flavor. Wild tea was a herb called tea weeds, which grew in the pasters and fields. You could either pull it green or pick it dry and put it in a paper sack. We collect it year round because it was also used for medicine for colds. For tea, take the leaves, put in boiling hot water, strain, sweeten, put in a fruit jar, cool, and drink. Vanilla flavor you mix with water to taste, sweeten, and drink hot or cold. The drinks were made two hours before a meal, put in a gallon jug or fruit jar, and let down a well or lay in a spring along the creek bed. Summer time the ice man come twice a week. The ice were wrap in news papers and hemp sacks or grass (burlap) sacks, which were use for sacking grain or cotton seeds and put in a tub in the coolest room in the house, which was usually the back bedroom where I slept. You would buy as much ice as the money could afford.

I remember whin I was a kid we would have been a lot more hungry some days if it had not been for a rabbit to eat. Even whin thing got better rabbit was welcome site on the table until the late forties whin the insecticide was introduce to the farmer, and the spraying of cotton for bugs and weed. It kill out the wild meat and the fresh wild fruits so what was once a meal to keep you from hungry become a meal for the volcher. Which become a bare spot on the ground.

To make myself clear the insecticide kill the small game rabbit, squirrel, and bird. The volcher-buzzard would eat the dead and in turn would die there. Any thing that die, the spot become a dead spot for a length of time. And then it become fertilize from the dead body and the spot would become a beautiful green spot.

I remember whin I would come home on leave from the Army during the late forties and the fifties. I would help Dad out on the farm. Whin I would see dead game in the field. I ask Dad who kill them and he said all this new poisoning we using these days. And you can't eat any thing out of the field. I remember asking Dad about the garden spot he all way had. He said any where you put a garden better be in your back yard. If you put it in the farm field you could not eat it after it was made ready beacause of the wide area of poison spray drifting from air plane and ground spray rigs. The garden spot that once made us a living on the farm soon was no more. The wild fruit trees disappear. The small game vanish and the big black clean-up bird vanish. That why in this part of the country you hardly ever see these animal or fowl.

Keep Clean

During my growing up days at school and at home sanatary was taught. In school we had a class period desenated to health. We learn how to brush our teeth and keep our body clean. You all no that most famley kept clean but there were some that did not keep clean nor keep the kids clean, so in school the teacher would teach kid how to keep clean, especial the girls.

At home mother was very strick on cleaness. First thing we were taught how to keep the house clean, wash dishes and food before cooking. Make sure your pans are clean.

People may not no this these days, that people did not take a bath every day back than. But in my home we keep clean by taking a bath at least two or three time a week. And it made no diffrent if you taken a bath at five in the evening, whin bed time come, you had to wash your face, hand, and feet. In the morning we brush our teeth and wash up or wipe down, whatever you want to call it. We never had any tooth paste so we use soda and salt to brush our teeth.

There were one thing for certain. Mother would not go or let anyone in the famley leave home without clean under ware, including Dad. If she had to wash our under clothes every night, she did. So that is one thing we were taught. She did not care about the outside, if the pants or dress was dirty or not. Of course Bessie would lie or try to say she had clean up. So Mother would check. And most of the time you could hear mother say, Get in there girl and wash up and put some clean clothes on. I'll be watching you, too.

It made no difference what come or go, did or be did, Bessie was involve in it. Whether it be good or bad. If thing were kind of sad around the house, Bessie could perk them up. If thing were good, Bessie could mess it up.

First thing we were taught how to keep the house clean, wash dishes and food before cooking. Make sure your pans are clean.

Sud Busting Day

I remember whin I was five or six we kid had to get up early on certain days. Wash day was one of those days. At night before wash day Mother would take the tub down to the well and fill the tub with water. And whin Dad come in from the field he had to come down the trail by the well to the house. So Mother would watch whin Dad start to the house. She would meet him at the well so he could help her carrie the tub of water. I remember this because while mother was drawing water we kid would play in the tub, or try to. Mother would say, Get outter my wash water. I don't want no dirt in it!

Whin we kids was growing up we were all way in my mom site—where ever she was we was, or in hollering distance. If she were busy and we kid were playing some place she would call up one by one by name until we answer. She had special concern on wash day. Everybody know of some kid, black or white, who got killed by falling in boiling wash pot. I guess that the concern she had, especial whin Bessie Lee was out of site.

Back to wash day. As I grew older and could draw water, around six year old, we kid all had to carrie water. We start a day before wash day hauling water. We all had bucket to fit the weight we could carrie. We would have to fill the three tub and two wash pot. One iron wash pot was for boiling clothes, the other pot to supply hot water as the wash water got cold. As mother wash and use water, we have to keep hauling it. Also get chips and stick of wood to keep the water hot in the iron wash pot. We also had to start the day before gathering chip and wood from the wood pile and stack it around the wash pot. We kid were not allow to fool around with fires until I was seven year.

Whin I was seven I remember this. Mother would say the night before wash day, garden day, and corn picking day, All

Mother would say the night before wash day, All right you kid, we got to rise and shine early in the morning.

right you kid, we got to rise and shine early in the morning. We got to either wash or go pick the ripe stuff in the garden or go pull corn roasten ears. Whin I first start making fire for wash day, Mom would tell Dad whin he got up to get me up so he can help Jr. get her wash water ready.

Mother all way felt that as I grew older I was responsible for what ever she had me to do. I thank my mother for that, so I grew up being responsible and trustworthy. Any way I could keep the fire going, and chug down clothes with old broom handle. Me and Mom could ring out the heavy clothes and I would hang them out. By the time I was ten all Mother had to say, Tomorrow is wash day. The reason she start preparing a day before, because if she did not have bluing, starch, and soap, I would have to hit the road and walk a mile and a half to the store.

Bluing was use to bleach out white clothes along with hanging them out side on a fence or a clothes line with the sunshine to purify and help bleach them.

By the time I was twelve me and my sister were doing all the washing and ironing. I would wash, Ruth would iron and Bessie Lee help hall water, and stay in the way. And I had to watch her to keep her out of the fire. She would try to take fire from around the wash pot and start another some other place.

I was sixteen whin we move close to Plano on Si and Vera Harrington place. Dad had left us. Mother work for Vera Harrington and once a week Mother, Ruth, and I wash and iron for Fred and Mrs. Callie Harrington for house rent, until I was eighteen whin I went into service.

The tubs was galvinise steel sizes numbers one, two, and three. Most famley would probly have four or five tub they use for washing, gathering garden and taking bath. In the summer every day we hall water, fill two tub or three. Leave them in the sun so the water could get hot. One tub was Dad, one for Mom and one for us kids. Bessie Lee being younger, she had to be last because she would splash all the water out. The only soap I see until I went in service was lye soap. Every once in a while we got a bar of palmolive soap and Mother would holler at us and say, Don't use all the soap. Save some for Dad.

I tell my family and young people today that there was no such thing as washing powder in my young days. And I had to wash and iron for house rent. And they think that was crazy. But that the truth.

48

If you want to look, feel, and smell some fresh sheets whin you wash them in your washing machine, try hanging them on the line in sunshine.

Recration or Play Time

I suppose all kid think of nothing but playing, and my growing up was the same. As I think back on those days I remember there were known games and there were creative games. I think I enjoy playing most whin mother would play with us.

There were never any store bought toys except maby on Xmas. There might be a Tom Mix or Lone Ranger cap gun for me and a doll for each of the girls. The girls all way got a black doll. Mother would help the girl make clothes for them. That was good for the girls because it taught them to sew. I'm sure it help Ruth. The size of famley she had, she had to make clothes. She still do a lot of sewing. I don't no about Bessie Lee. She didn't take time to do any thing but tear up and stir up trouble.

In winter whin we could not go outside, or after school, we play jacks, pitty pat cards, and dominoes. We had Chinese checkers. All five of us would play at once. My Dad and I would play checkers while my mother and sisters play jacks. Some time we could get mother to play hide in seek. If there were snow we get old tubs, tires, boxes and use for sled. We would push each other and slide down the hill behind our house. If the water in the stream was froze hard enough we would skate on the icy stream. There was a lot more snow then than now.

During the spring and summer it were plenty of outside game we did. We play stick ball. Mother would stuff rag in a sock. We would use broom stick for bat. We choose side—two against two. We call it stick ball or rag ball.

We would use old tires, what we call casings, ball ourself up into the casing and the other would roll us down a hill. We would take chopping hoe and push around like it was a car or truck. We made swing on a tree limb with rope or chain and tire. We climb trees—me and Bessie Lee. Ruth was more of a

We would use old tires, what we call casings, ball ourself up into the casing and the other would roll us down a hill.

house girl. We did not have much trouble finding thing to do with Bessie Lee. She was tough as boot leather and would do any thing or get into any thing. Bessie Lee was the type that Mother had to watch her like a chickin watch a hawk. Bessie and I would catch grass hopper, tie the thread on their legs and hook a penny match box, and play like the grass hopper is a horse and the box a wagon. We would put as much dirt in the box as the grass hopper could pull. We catch butter fly, tie a string and paper on the leg, and turn it aloose and watch it fly away. We would take coat hanger and stiff wire, bend a hook in the wire and roll little iron wheels. We would swing like monkey and play Tarzan in the mule barn. We play tag. One would touch the other, and the other had to tag you back or tag some one else. It was all way more fun whin there were more kids just to see who got the last tag.

At night we would catch lightning bug and smear them on the wall or a post to make it look like a town. We would give the town a name. Depending on how many lightning bug you smear up would be the name of the town—like Plano, Dallas, McKinney, and so on. The bugs would die whin we smeared them but the light would last a while.

Fishing was a good recration, and us kid could play in the water, take small flat rock and throw them on the water to make them skate or skip on to see which one could make them go the farest.

The older men like my Dad would have dog races. Men would gather together with gray hounds, go where the jack rabbit were, find one setting in the bed, line the dog up, and some one would ease up to the rabbit and scare it up. Whin it got a distance away the men would have made their bets and off the dog would go. Whin they unsnap the chain every body would be hollering, Sick em, Go get em. There were much fun to have as a famley.

Some of the best fun as a group was 19th June and picnick. There were plenty of kid to play with, ball game, racing, swimming, who could eat corn on the cob fastest, spitting water melon seeds. There were no prizes—just fun. Whin the country famleys got together it was friendly, and a lot to gossip about after the eating. Men got together for cards, dominoes, checkers, shooting at target with .22 rifles to see who could shoot the best. I think my Dad all way won.

The women would get together and me, I was the nosey type. I try to play with kids and slip around to see and hear what the older one were talking about. The women would be saying thing like this, Girl, did you see so and so with so and so? Or, Child, did you no so and so is having another baby and it ain't his either? Well, whose is it? I don't no. It could be any body. She all way flirting with some body.

The men, on the other hand, would talk boxing, base ball, or how hard they would work harvesting grain in order to go to the June Teenth Shang Dang (good party). Some would say, Man, that white man work the hell out of us last week.

There was one big farm owner in the area would all way wait until just before June Teenth to start harvest grain just so the colored hands on his farm could not go to June Teenth.

There were all way a lot of fun at the June Teenth until some of the suppose to be city slick party goers drop in half drunk and try to start trouble, cursing, loud talk and just be known as plain old hell raising. Some time there would be fight brake out. It would not last long. The farm men would run them off. The June Teenth Shang Dang were held down in Dr. Dye woods along the White Rock Creek. The June Teenth finally play out until recent years whin the Blacks have started it going again.

Medicines

Doctors and medicine was out of the question in my young days. I only went to the doctor two time before I reach the age of eighteen—once whin I was scalded with hot water, and once whin my leg was broke. My home was quarantee once whin I was seven or eight because my sisters had scarlet fever, but I never did.

My young sister was very dangerous and destructive while I cooked breakfast. One morning whin I was ten or eleven I fryed my two sisters eggs and I boiled mine. We had got a three burner oil stove. While standing over my boiling egg I called my sisters and said, Don't you wish you had boiled your eggs. Come see how my eggs are boiling.

My young sister were too short to see in the pot, so she grab the stove to pull up and see. The stove tip over and the pot of boiling water flip right on my chest. I had a T shirt on. I grab and begin to pull off my shirt and all the skin came with it. The deepest spot was in the holler of my right chest pit and ran down in the shape of a hump back camel. My sister never got a drop of water.

By the time my two sister went up in the field and found my dad, I was out in the middle of the paster in much pain. My dad came to the house and settle me down and had to run about two mile to get a car and my mother at work at Jessie Haggard's. We finely got to the Doc Wyatt in Plano. He clean me up and use some type of salve on my burn. This was right after Easter.

Six month later my young sister did it again. It was cotton picking time. My shoulder scar had not heal yet. We was picking cotton at the home place behind John Wells barn. The truck was loaded and it was lunch time. All the hands was walking up to the house to eat where it was shade trees and cool well water. Anybody did not have lunch, Momma Wells would feed them. The three of us, me and my two sisters, rode with a driver name Vaxter, and about the same time my young sister lean over and open the truck door and out I went. The ground was soft but the truck wheel ran over my right leg and broke it. Back to Doctor Wyatt. He reset my leg and put it in a cast. Another six month, with sore burns and broke leg.

That the only times I ever went to a doctor. There all way seem to be some type of home made remedies or medicine if some one got sick. My dad would get the chills a lot of times. He kept a medicine call 3-666 and Mother would heat bricks and a clothes iron and wrap them up, put them in bed with Dad, pile all cover on him, and get in bed with him. It all way work. In an hour or two he would be like a new man.

Whin my sisters had the scarlet fever they were very sick. Mother then did not know what was wrong. They sent to town for Dr. Wyatt. Whin he arrived he discovered it was scarlet fever. He gave quinine and suggested sheep ball tea. Mother had me gather sheep balls—those that were dry. She would put them in boiling water with a little sugar and we had to drink it for head and chest cold.

Doctor left instructions that no one was to leave out of the paster surrounding this house for ten to fifteen days. Of course Dad paid this no attention. He said he had to go work, and he went. So we was stuck behind the fence, mom and the three of us. This was during warm weather whin Mom, usually whin she was feeling blue, would grab her poles and head for the creek. She would all way say, I'm going fishing where I can have some peace.

She would make it clear to Bessie Lee, I don't want no trouble out of you today. Usually Bessie Lee knowed whin Mom mean business and not play with bait and pull fish out of the pail. But this was quarantee and we was stuck.

There was things that we needed and Dad would tell Mr. Ray and he would get rice, beans, flour, corn meal, maybe some medicine and bring them up to the gate which was about a quarter mile from our house. He would honk or somebody would be watching and we kids would take off running. Mom would holler, Don't you all strow that stuff up and down the road.

There were other home remedies beside sheep ball tea whin we were ailing. Dad would make us a lemon stew—boil the lemon, put Vicks salve in and whiskey, and we would drink it as hot as you could stand it. Then we would get a rub down on our chest, back, throat and nose, go to bed, cover up, and sweat it out. Usually two time like this and we were OK. We never did have to miss school. Some time there were pepper mint candy and whiskey dissolve in a fruit jar and use for cough medicine. Cow chip tea, wild tea, and crow soup for cold and fever. (Crow meat was use for colds more often than chicken. It also serve as a meal, with corn bread.) Cole oil or karseen in sugar for croope, termentine in sugar good for aches, pain, and sore muscles. Karseen use for cut and bruse.

There was not near as much sickness in my young days as it is this day and time. I think I can attribute that to some of the old home made remedies and the cold winters that killed out germs and fertilize the ground with nitrogen from the snow. Also the only insecticide used was sulphur. Dad used to walk up and down the cotton rows at night dusting with sulphur, cranking a little auger machine strapped around his neck. Potatoes and cabbage were also dusted with sulphur. But that was all. So food was more eatable.

I was asmatic. There were no doctor or medicine a poor family could buy for asma. I think I had it about as bad as a kid growin up could get. Whinever I would get asma attact my Mother and Dad would lay my head and chest over their knee and start beating my back. I would be hassling for breath some time for an hour. They rubbing and beating my back. When ever I could get a good breath, I or they would stick a finger down my throat to make me throw up. Once the slime and flem broke up, and once I throw up, I would feel fairly well but tired. So I would go to sleep and rest. Technology and research have trace asma to your genes. A certain type of dust, grain dust, was my worse trouble for asma. One reason, we kids love to play in the barn where the grain was stored. There were times whin they would heat hot water, put Vicks salve in it and while it was steaming put a towel over your head and you inhale the steam and it work very well.

For cut you use smutt from the stove, castor oil, and Black Draught for constipation and colds.

I recall how we kids use to find wasp nest and throw rock and stick at it. And how the bumble bee would make hive in the ground under the out door toilet. And the chicken would lay egg under the toilet. Between gathering the egg and throwing stick to knock down wasp nest, I would stir up the bumble bee and all way get stung. The first thing Mother would do to doctor the sting was look for some tobacco or snuff to moisten it and rub on. If there were none she would get the bluing and blot on the sting and it certain work fine to stop the stinging and help stop the swelling.

I remember how Mother would not wash without bluing to help with the bleaching of clothes. There were other uses too. We would use it for color pitcher. On rainy day Mother would say, Lets color something. She would put bluing in a cup or top and we would dip our finger in the cup and make drawings on paper sack and card borde from grocery store. Bluing may not have cost that much but there were not much money to spend. Mother did not care about me and Ruth using the bluing, but every time Bessie Lee get hurt or stung she would run for the

Every time Bessie Lee get hurt or stung she would run for the bluing
bottle. Mom would hear her and holler out, Don't waste it.
Bring it here. I'll put it on.

bluing bottle. Mom would hear her crying and holler out, Don't
you fool with that bluing. You ain't gonner do nothing but waste
it. And I ain't got none to waste. Don't open it. Bring it here. I'll
put it on.

That the story of bluing use for medicine, coloring and
decoration.

School Day

I were the smart one with the dumb idea.

I don't really know if the kids these day are any diffrent than the days I were growing up. Probly the oppitunity are better now than they were whin I grew up. Studying habits are the same. Parents still have to make kids get their home work and try to make them understand education is the best thing for you. For me whin I was going to school my greatest ambition was to get a good education. But at the same time my dumbest idea were to get a education without studying. I soon learn better. I guess I was pretty dumb in school because of the four wall. I could never think very well whin I was box in. Or let me say force to do something even if it was for my own good.

My sister were much diffrent. Ruth were the smartest of us all. Bessie Lee was smart enough to get by. She was good at doing things and studying but did it only whin she had to. Mother had to keep us seperated doing our home work. Bessie Lee would not let no body do any. She could find the most unusual thing to do to interrupt your study even if she was on the other side of the house. She would do thing like start coughing out loud and continue. She would whisle, sing, or keep calling some body. Even at school she had to be put by her self. Most of the time she had to sit by the teacher. My biggest problum was whin I got old enough to go to school, Mother had all ready taught us the school basics: counting, time tables to the threeses, and reading.

We learn to read at school but also at home and Church and Sunday School. Many of the grown folks did not know how to read. Those who did probly learned from Bible reading at home. Famleys read the Bible together every night before bed time and then have prayer. At our house every body would get on ther knees, except Dad who was respectful but might be

59

rolling a cigerette. During my young days Mother would pick out scriptures in the Bible and begin to read. Then she would tell one of us kid to pick up where she left off from. The words we could not pronounce she would spell them out and pronounce and say, You spell it and pronounce it. Ruth could always pronounce good. I was hard to learn and Bessie Lee, you had to make her learn.

Not only in the homes did you learn how to read but there was prayer meeting where every body were taught to read. The leader would call on almost any body to read a scripture, lead a song, or pray. It was embarrassing to some of the peoples who could not read or did not want to pray or did not know the song. Then some body sitting close would say, Go ahead. I'll help you. Some body would pass the Bible or hymn book to the person and some one beside them read or sing with them. There were some the next week who would overcome their shyness and before many weeks would be leading songs. Most everybody went to Church and Sunday School and prayer meeting, so it was a advantage to young parents who had not finish school to have members of the church help in this way. The elders who could not read might think they were too old to learn but they insist on the young ones being taught at church.

The school I went to I think have a problum being identified by some peoples. The school may have had a diffrent name before I went to it, but as long as I can remember, the school and church I went to was call Shepton Colored School and Shepton Church. This building was across Preston Road and 500 yards to the west of the road. It was bout forty feet by thirty feet. It face south and had one door and a porch all the way across the front. There were windows down both sides and in front. No windows in the back. Inside in the back there were a platform three feet by five feet and a podium which stay in the place all the time. The teachers four leg table that sit in front of the platform and podium were use for the teacher desk. I don't remember any book or library kept there. The teacher had a foot locker in her car with books. The books that we had were old and raggy. And I can remember whin Mr. Sigler would bring use books out to the school at Shepton. All the book I ever got was all ready torn up. The cover were off. Leaf were missing.

One thing about going to school in my school days: you were taught very good. What you learn usually stuck with you. Each grade were divided up in groups and to this day I don't see how the teacher taught thirty or thirty-five kids, grades from the first to seventh. I think it was the home work you had to take home and bring back every day and the determination of the kids and the parents, along with a leather strap.

Audrey Thornton was the only teacher I remember until her last year, seventh grade. She drove her Dad Cadillac car and carry her book and school work in a big bag to and for home every day. And the last year whin she was going to have a baby, the seventh grade was taught by her husband, Lucius Davis, who was a teacher out of Dallas.

There were a boy and girl toilet out on a rocky hill. Two basket ball goles. And they did have a basketball team! It would be mix with older boys who had finish and school boys. We play teams like Frisco, Cilina, Rock Hill, White Rock, and Carlton. The school had two cole burning stoves. In winter the kids would take turns standing around the stove to keep warm. School would start one month early for a month and then turn out for kid to go pick cotton. Hours of school were from 8:00 to 4:00. There were wheat field around the school. Every year old man Fred would come down to school and tell Audry to keep the kids out of the fields. We knock down too much wheat.

Regular school were broke down in two session. We start to school in August and again in September or October. Thats because of cotton picking time. And for most famleys, country and city, cotton picking time were the only time whin you could make any money. The whole family got involve in picking cotton. You pick five and a half day a week. Then on Saturday evening were the best time of our life. We got to go to town. Pretty often during cotton picking we got that one pair of church and school shoes, two pair of Long John, two shirt, maybe three. And two or three duckings (overalls)—two for school and one for church—paper, colors, and cedar pinsel and tablets for school.

One thing I found out at a early age while going to school is there were only very few select black farm kids that got to finish high school or even think about college. The country school only went to the sixth or seventh grade and if a black farm kid were able to get through those grades, that were all the education they got because there was no way to town. Mostly farm kid made it through the fifth grade and that was it.

I think I was very fortunate to be able to finish school. One reason was whin I finish the sixth grade Dad gave up share cropping and we move to Allen on the Moore farm where we had 300 acre to work and Moore gave Dad all he could make on the farm. But that another story. I started to school in Allen. I was going to the seventh grade. About half way through the seventh I had to quit school and work the farm, so I flunk the seventh grade and by the time the next school year started and the crops were ready to harvest, Dad move us back to Ray Haggard place.

Any way Shepton School only went to the sixth grade and about that time Plano had gave Plano Colored School a bus and we started to school in Plano. I had to start all over in the seventh grade, but I was smart enough to catch up to the eighth grade and that is how I got to finish High School. All of

Shepton Colored School. One thing about going to school in
my days: you were taught very good.

my other education I got was self study courses I taken on my
own in the army. Whin I got out of the army I went to Richland
College and Grayson County College. I still lack a few hour
from getting my degree in personell business management.
Again I taken up farming and again farming stop me from
getting an education. Maybe soon if I can give up some of my
fishing pleasure I'll go back to school.

Again I say it was hard for a farm family with kids to get a
high school deploma. My sister Ruth, as smart as she was, only
got to the tenth grade and Bessie Lee got through the ninth
grade. Out of all of my Shepton school mates that stayed on the
farm, none never did finish school. If I can remember, Shepton
School close about 1946 or 1947. I would have to look up the

record to be sure. Audrey, the teacher, got pregnant and retired I think about that time. I don't even no where any of my Shepton school mates is these days. If any body no any Shepton school kid of the 1935 to 1945 time, please get in touch with Eddie Stimpson, 1000 F Avenue, Plano, Texas 75094. Phone (214) 423-3767. Thank you.

After School Trouble

I suppose there is times whin people take thing for granted, even my self, but down through the years I learned that obidiance pay off. Here is some things I have thought about for years and more as I get older and this is what it is. There must be one of the strongest ties in the world between mother and child. In my case I no it was. I can remember as plain as day that every time there were some thing bother me or worrie me my mother would sense if there were danger in front of my day to day activities. She would detect it and remind me not to go or do a certain thing. During my growing up years from the time I was big enough, and my dad taught me to hunt and my mother and grandmother taught me to fish, they could not keep me off the creek fishing or out of the woods hunting. There are a cupple of time I can recall that mother stop me and others from possible serious damage to my life as well as some one else.

The time was late in the fall. I had a fight in school and I think it was one of the most serious and damage fight in my young years. It was noon one day at school that I had a argument with a girl. By two-thirty recess I had forgot about it. But not the girl. I was standing on the ground leaning on the porch post whin some thing hit me over the head. My knees buckle. Stars cloud and tears come into my eyes. All I could see for a moment as I regain my self there stood the girl with a baseball bat cocked and ready to swing again. I come to my senses and grab the bat to snatch it. She was holding the bat tight and whin I snatch she fall into the post and I grab her with my hand and lock my arm around her and the post and latch on to her like a dog latch onto a piece of meat. I bit down on her jaw and held on with the intention of biting a plug out. Whin I no any thing the teacher was pulling me off saying, Boy,

Don't you no better than to fight a girl. Get on out to the toilet and cool off.

By this time I no what I plan to do whin school turn out at 3:30. After school I rush home, got the .22 rifle, told mother I was going hunting, like I did every day. She said, Ok, be back before dark.

Out the door I went. I headed down cross the paster toward the route of the girl I had the fight with, with the intention of killing her I was so angry. I was all most in a trot whin all of a sudden there was a voice came from behind me saying, Come on back to the house Eddie Jr., and right then I no my mother no that I was up to some thing no good. I froze in my track whin mother said, Give me the gun, and ask me what was the matter. And I begin to tell her all the detail and what I was going to do. And the most frighten thing came into my mind was I knew she would tell Dad and I would be grounded from using the gun to go hunting. I think Mom and Dad gave one of the most serious talking to I've had in my life time. To this day I remember most of what they taught me about premeditation and the use of a gun or anything else you would do whin you had time to think about it.

What had happen? My ways and action whin I got home that day was no diffrent from any other day, I thought, but mother had felt, caught or detect some thing was not right.

Any way they did not ground me from hunting, but it did make them aware and remind me to let them no whin and where I was going to hunt. If there is any thing I can remember well, that is remember day in and day out, the care and concern Mother had for us kids and Dad. It didn't make no diffrence whin or what time it was. Every time one of us walk out that door Mother wanted to no where we were going and what time would we be back. It was the same if mother left the house. She say she be back at a certain time. It was a bit diffrent with us if she no where we were going. She would take time and caution us what danger was ahead especial going across the road, to the store or creek to play in water. She had a safety tip for us all. Every day Dad go to work I could hear her say, Eddie. You be careful on that tractor. Watch them old horses. You be careful with them guns, whin we go hunting. Make sure we don't shoot each other. I can give Mother a lots of praises for this caution and safety. Of course it did not matter with sister Bessie Lee. She was going to do something wrong, time she got out of Mom site. Any way this is why Mom would all way say, You be good Bessie Lee. Eddie Jr., keep a eye on that child. Bessie Lee all way wanted to foller me around and a lot of time I'd take her hunting with me with mother permission. Mom would all way say, You stay close to Eddie Jr., girl.

Hussling for Survival

As far back as I can remember work was part of my famleys every day living. Starting back whin, I was told that my Dad had work all his life. Whin his family move to Plano from the country, he move in with his uncle and family. There he work for room and board. He did as all other kid at an early age— chop wood, help in the fields. He learn how to farm, such thing as how to harness and hitch up a team of horses, he learn to plant and set the plows to plow corn and cotton. He learn about counting acres in a field. At twelve year old he went out on his own with Ray Haggard. He raise his first crop as a share cropper. The money he made on cotton the first year went to his mother Corie Stimpson. I think it was about $180. His mother put a roof on her house. That about all I learn about what Dad did that so special at that age.

Ray say he could all way depend on Pete (what he call my dad) to get the job did. By the age of fifteen he was often used as a straw boss, even to some of the older men. A straw boss was responsible for keeping drinking water, sharpening chopping hoes, moving from one field to another and the welfare of the hands. The word "hands" mean the peoples the straw boss is in charge of to see the job is did right.

A straw boss would be glad to see the big boss ride up on his horse and hear a few word of how good a job they are doing or even how bad, or maby you need a tool, but could not go get it. We was all way glad whin Mr. Ray or Johny Ray rode up and we welcome them.

You may have two or more straw boss on one farm depending on how many job going on. Look at it this way: You have the boss who is the owner, the straw boss, and assistant. Today you have president, vice president, superviser, foreman, and secretary. One good thing about the old days—you didn't have ten people to go through to get to the boss.

Dad help support his family and his self until he got married. This is where my mother took up the slack. She began raising a garden and kept ther cotton field clean. Whin I was old enough, I remember the grass sack they made for me to help pick cotton. Whin my sister were born Mother would take us to the field where Ruth would ride on the cotton sack that Mother dragged. Some time whin the sack got full the baby would roll off, mother would stomp a holler in the cotton sack and lay the baby in till she got about thirty to fifty pound and go weigh it. Whin Bessie Lee were born Mother some time had to drag both the girls on the sack. Ruth were big enough to walk but would get tired.

By the time I got six or seven I were a big help. Chop wood, cook the beans and corn bread, feed the chickin and turkey, feed the hogs corn, and put corn out for the horses and mules. That would help Dad out. All he had to do is unharness the horses and go to the house. Whin all the cotton were pick, my Mother and us kid would go scrapping cotton. Scrapping cotton was picking up cotton that was wasted, pull the few bolls that open late and a little piece of cotton left in a cotton burr. We would all way make enough to buy our school clothes and shoes. We would scrap until it rain or got too cold—usually until Christmas. Mother would save enough out to buy her Christmas baking needs.

During the winter the men would cut wood for home use and sell about once a month. They would load up a wagon, leave early in the morning going to Plano where they sold the wood and split the money. There would be my Uncle Ronney, my cousin Almond Drake, whose nickname was Fat or Tank. I guess I make my first dollar helping saw, chop, and load wood at about eight or nine years old. We also hussle and pick up scrap iron. We kid and mother no that was pretty good money.

69

When my sister were born Mother would take us to the field where
Ruth would ride on the cotton sack that mother dragged.
Some time whin the sack got full the baby would roll off, mother
would stamp a holler in the sack and lay the baby in.

During the summer months Ray Haggard would all way
come by the house, drive up to the gate. We kid would run out
to meet him. He would give my sister a nickle or dime and ask
my mother could I go with him. He call and say, Millie, can
June Bug ride with me? Mother would all way say yes. He use
me to open and close the gate or that day I would go with him

he would go to every paster or field he had stock and ride through the herd of cow and count them, the same as sheep. Some farmers had goats running with the sheep. They were good to lead the sheep from one place to another. I would stay all day with Ray. We would go by the store. He would buy my pop, candy, and feed me a sandwich. Whin he bring me back that evening he would drop me off at the gate of the paster I live in, give me some money, and thank me. I all way took mother the money.

My next hard earn money was building fence. I was thirteen or fourteen and made seventy-five cents a day. It was hard work because we had to take a crow bar to chip though the rock deep enough to put a post level with the other. We use bord'arc and cedar post and barb wire.

My third earn money was chopping cotton. They said I was old enough to work as a half a hand. I was paid sixty-two and a half cents a hour. I did not like it. I told them so and I quit. If I could do the same work as the grown up, I wanted my pay.

Lets go back to cotton picking. I was never able to pick cotton. Mother would give me a quarter to pick that day and I could never pick over a hundred pound. The most unbearable thing I remember about picking cotton was early one morning whin I was ten or eleven year old. There were no dew. My Uncle Ronney ask my mother could I pick with him that day. He was going to learn me how to pick cotton. She said yes. And oh boy I think she regretted it for days. My uncle and I started out picking snatch row. I was on the right side of him. You straddle one row on the outside, and snatch all you can of the middle row. My uncle were use to picking seven to nine hundred pound a day in good cotton. This was good cotton. By the end of the day I had pick three hundred pound and he had about a thousand pound.

I think I had to crawl home. With Mom help I went to bed

71

without eating and could not rest or even hardly move. The next morning I could not get up. For two day I had to stay in bed. My mother would rub me down, put hot pad and hot iron and brick on me to draw the soreness out. That was the way I graduate from the cotton patch. I did not put on another cotton sack.

I had learn enough about math so I keep books and weigh cotton for every body who work in the field that day. Whin the truck or wagon got 1800 or 2000 pounds on it, it was a bale of cotton. If any body wanted ther money that day, I would figger ther pound and pay. And Ray Haggard at quitting time would drive up with a sack of money and would ask, June Bug, does anybody want ther money today?

After the cotton were pick I was good with horses and mules. I was made a field hand cutting stalks, plowing, planting, braking ground. I could catch my own team of horses and harness it and hook them up to whatever machinery were going to be use. Whin Ray got his first lug wheel tractor I learn very fast to operate it. By fifteen I was a full farm hand following in Dad foot steps. I had to go through the fifth grade and the seventh grade twice because I had to work to help support the family, working with farm animal and farm work from braking the ground, planting the seed, and harvest the crop. It's not too much I don't no. I may not no it all but most of farming I no—from the horse and mule days to the modern equipment days.

I think my family was very fortunate by my Dad ability to start out early in life as a farmer, and to have a boss man like Ray Haggard. There were never no money, but there were hand me down clothes, and plenty of garden space to grow food. I use to wonder where were the money since we work all the time. But I soon found out all the money we made was paid to cover what had been borrow to keep the car running and thing we need in winter whin there were not much work.

It was years before my Dad learn this, until he and my Mother sit down and talk it over on what to do. For a year we did without to see if it would work. They did not borrow any money and Dad and Mom would lay the crop by and go to other farms and work. We were fortunate enough to have a boss like Ray who did not care that whin all the work on his place were finish we could go to work some other place. Most of the other area farmers would not let his colored hand go and work some place else.

And some farmers, no matter how hard or how good a worker you are, all way had a way to keep you from getting ahead in finance or moving away from his farm by keeping you in debt. Now, by not borrowing money and by working extra on neighboring farms, we were able to stay out of debt. We couldn't save but we were debt free. It was then in 1944 we moved to Allen. Until now I have puzzled over why we didn't stay, but that another story.

I was working all my life as a farm hand. Whin I went into the army in 1948, I was a farm hand for Quentin Robinson and Miss Ammie Wilson. I came out of service in 1969, as a sargeant, and work as a farm hand with my dad for a while with Cyril Carpenter and the Wells Brother until 1986. I still had no money. I made as a farm hand just enough to get by or work by week and sometime not even enough. I guess if I had to do farming all over I would love the farming. So if I had to do all the ups again I suppose:

> Get up
> Wash up
> Eat up
> Run up the horses
> Feed up

73

Catch up the horses
Harness up the horses
Hook up to the plow or wagon
And then you say, Geddie up
After that you may have to pick up rocks
Pull up the corn
Fill up the wagon
And empty up
Put up the horses
Go up to the house
Wash up
Eat up
And go up to bed

And that day in and day out if you a farm hand. Why don't you try it some time, if you can find a mule or if you smart enough to drive a tractor.

Sending Messages without a Phone

Most message as I remember were carried or transport by the boss man or woman of the farm you stay on, and that made every body no what every body no, so it was hard to keep any secret. There were cars, telephone, horse back. The most prompt message were the white rag—big enough to see for miles. There were plenty of open space on the farms and to send a message from farm famley to farm famley, if there were a emergency such as death or sickness, some one would get up on a hill or in a clearing where they could see the other house or the field where you were working, and wave the white rag until some one would notice and wave back a white rag. And on and on, house to house and field to field. Sometimes the message would travel real fast if there were peoples in every field working.

I remember one incident whin a lady were very sick and died, the message were sent by a white sheet from the famley to our famley to find out what was wrong. Once you got the white rag signal some one would go to that famley before the day was over to see what was wrong. If some of your famley in town was in trouble some of the white peoples would call the other and the other would call the other until the message got to you. Most of the country farm famley had a car or horse to transport message. Eventual every body would get told. These days even with all the modern message technology, if some thing happen next door you still don't no. In the old days people had much more responsibility and concern about one another famleys.

One message my family got that was very important was in the early or mid 1940s. The movie gave away money every Tuesday night, if you register and your name was drawn. My name was drawn one Tuesday night in 1944. The flood had

75

If there were a emergency such as death or sickness, some one would get up on a hill or in a clearing where they could see the other house or field, and wave the white rag until some one would notice.

came a week before. After twenty-four inches had fell in twelve hours, all the bridges were wash out between my home and Plano. We had to go all the way down Preston Road through Renner and Richardson to get to Plano. So about 11:00 that night Ray Haggard and his family came by and told us my name was drawn for seventy-five dollar, and I could go get it. About 12:00 my Uncle Grady came all the way round from Plano to tell us. They stay on Si and Vera Harrington farm and had to go all the way back around to ther home.

And that was the concern people had for each other—white and black. It not like that today. It dog eat dog or get the message the best way you can, especial if it a benefit to you. If it gossip or some thing to get you in trouble you can hear it the next minute and it been told in ten diffrent way whin you really get the truth. So if you are cautious you hear little, see little, and believe none until you know the fact. End of message. Keep your white sheet handy. It a sure truth. Keep your eyes open and answer back to acknowledge the message. Then respond.

I remember whin we would go to the fields and every body got ready to start chop or pick, some one in the group would ask if any body got the white rag just in case we got a message. If no body did, one kid would be sent back to the house for a white rag about two foot by two foot or four foot by four foot.

Domestic Animals

Horses, mule, cows, hog, goats, sheep, chicken, turkey, duck, goose, pigeon. There may be many other, but these are the animals I my self is most familiar with. Each animal has a distinction of it own.

Cow can be about as wild as any animal I know if a man or some one is not around them all the time. All cow can become a milk cow after ther first calf but you have to train them, and even the best train milk cow will some time kick you and your milk over while you have them in a stall. To prevent this you put leg hobble on. Also each cow no ther own stall where they eat and be milk. Cow are very good mother and very protective of the herd they with. During the day or night whin the calf are fed, the cows will bed down ther babies and at least one mother cow will stay there with them.

A cow have a steady feeding habit. The only time they are not eating is whin they are lying down or some thing unusual enter the field where they are, such as dog, deer, hogs, a strange person, even rabbits. They will stand still in ther track and watch what ever it is until it out of site or come too close to ther position, and if this happen they have a certain bellow and all take up a defense position, putting all the young in the middle or between them and the danger.

You halter them, learn them to be led, pet them, groom and keep them at a balance diet. You learn them not to be frighten of any thing. Once you train them as a pet and show calf you can't let them back out in ther pasture with the other stock. They become easy prey to predators or ther own will fight and kill them. From the show they are usually taken to a slaughter house and kill for market purpose.

Sheep were a very special animal. It was use for several purpose and easy prey to dogs and wolf. So every night they had to be fasten up in a barn lot and fed oats. What I remember about sheep is during lamb season and shearing the wool. During lamb birth there were all way some young ewes that probly would need help having the lamb. You had to be careful because the mother may reject the lamb. Whin this happen you fasten them both up in a tight pen and some time you had to hold the mother sheep to let the baby suck until she get use to it.

Sheep shearing was all way profible for me. Whin the sheep shearer would come I would go out where a sheep had died, gather the wool remaining and sell it to the buyer. Some time the shearmen would buy the remain. If not we could take it to the cotton gin in Kamy or Plano and sell the wool. Wool would sell like cotton. If the market was good, you sell. If the market was bad you wait for the price go up.

Between a hog and chicken you would have to flip a coin to see which one the nastiest. My dad and I have raise hog as long as I can remember. If you are raising hogs for the market, in six month from birth they should weigh from 190–230 pound. If you are raising them for meat hogs for your famley, you may keep them until they get 300–500 pound. Out of a 500 pound you will probly get five to ten gallon of lard.

Hog killing was very special, and we would all way kill hog twice during winter, before Christmas and in February. There were all way two or three family kill hog together. The men would start the fire, get the vat or barrel ready for scalding, sharpen knifes. The women would be sewing sausage sacks. The kids were able bring up fire wood but usually stack it close to the pot. If you were old enough to put wood on the fire, some one would tell you whin and what side to put it on. There were all way other kid around and a close eye were on them at all time.

From the time the hog was gutted open, the liver and

tenderloin were strip out and some of the women would start frying some meat. Some women and me would start cleaning the guts for chittlings. The most remember thing I like about the hog killing was the lard cook out. Once the lard was cook out, we kids could dig in the cracklings and eat. During hog killing time there were all way plenty of help. Work in the field were lay by for winter. Hog killing is a very remember thing to me as a kid. It was fun. It was exciting the way they shot the hog between the eyes and then cut the throte and stab the heart to bleed. The hot water had to be a certain tempature and the ashes from the fire was used to help cut the hair while scraping the hide. After scraping, they would split the hind foot, pull out the strong leaders, and hook the trace hook in leader and hoist the hog up on a frame. A frame is three poles stood up, tied at the top, then spread open in tryangle. Once the hog is strung up, it is wash down and finish draining, then gutted open and then block out in four pieces and then trim out. While one or two men block and trim out, the other men will be cutting up lard and sausage meat. If you have ever did any hog killing I guess one never forget. This is Febuary 1991 and I just kill two hogs. It brought back many remember.

I suppose one of the most remarkable animal this country ever seen, had, or use is the mule. It is sad to no that the very thing God put on this earth for man to make a living and build this country with were brutely used up and throwed away and made dog food, while in some country it is call a delicacy food. Whin modern equipment began to roll onto the farm field, those team of mule would began to disappear until finally there were no mule to be seen in this part of the state. I would be willing to bet that kids from thirty or thirty-five years old down, to this day and time have never seen a mule unless maby at a movie or maby a horse show or fair.

But I remember from the time I was able to crawl into a

wagon with my dad or uncle and hold the line of a team of mule. I was taught to respect a mule because they had as much sense as you did and you had to all way let them no who were the boss and in control. Other wise there were two thing they would do: run away once they was hook up to a wagon or plow, or balk and not even move whin you try to make them go. It would be like a see saw with each other and not going any where. Once a team get this stubborn mood it nothing you can do but take a brake until they are ready to move. This would only happen if the team of mule no that you were not in control.

I remember the first time my dad and uncle ask if I want a team of mule. I didn't no they were for real. But whin they ask me if I can catch and harness the team they point out to me, my face lite up like a Christmas tree. I suppose my dad no or had confidence that I could. But little did he or the rest no that I probly had more control of the mule than they did. Remember I feed them every day, I petted them daily, they ate out of my hand, I would catch them out in the middle of the paster and ride them bare back some time. I had to lead them in a ditch to get on ther back. I had a lot of practice unhooking the team and taking off the harness.

So I caught the two they point out. They were the biggest in the lot I thought. At least they were older and tamer. The only problum I had was throwing the harness over ther back and fit it over the collar, but I lead them up to the feed trough and harness them up and hook them to a bull rake to rake cotton stalks into a winrow. Even after school I would go catch, harness up, hook up, and go up to the field and work until dark.

I'm sure people think all horses and mule are broke like the cowboy broke riding horses. No, you are wrong. Working horses and mule are broke with one or two other trained horses or

A large horse or mule owner would probly have ten or fifteen working teams, and diffrent team for diffrent work.

mule. Whin you have got them tame down or what you call barn or pen broke and able to catch, you begin to put harness on them day by day for a while. Then you begin to leave the harness on half or all day. Then you hook the horse or mule between another trained pair and lead them around, then hook them to a wagon or plow and work them until they are ready for field work. A large horse and mule owner would probly have ten or fifteen working team and diffrent team for diffrent work—some to plant, some to plow, row crop like cotton and corn, and the big and strong teams for braking ground.

It a beautiful site whin you look out in a field and see ten team of mules working, like looking at a pitcher. People traveling along Preston Road would stop and look and take a pitcher of a man and his team plowing. I can tell you this, the same big machines in the farm field producing the food that you eat every day is the same food that build America, only it was horse and mule that began to bring us where we are now. In recent years historian society have tryed to preserve the mule and jack ass and donkeys.

On this subject you will have to use your imagination because there are two aspect to look at. The first is modern equipment. If you line up ten tractor with the attached equipment in a hundred acre field, it would only take about a hour to clean the hundred acre farm field. Now let us use our imagination using this same hundred acre field. And line up ten team of horses and mule with that equipment and start out the same time. In about one hour you would hardly have made a round or went from one end and back where you started. But like any thing some team are faster than the other. In two hour all ten team with attached plow would be scattered up and down the hundred acre. It may take a week or more to finish this field with a team instead of one hour with a tractor.

But I can remember how beautiful it looks whin you stop along the highway, as many traveler did to just sit and look and take pitcher day in and day out. What make this pitcher so beautiful is to see how graceful those team pull the plows and how those men would handle the team with experience, working ability and the control they had over the team.

I can remember well as those team of horses and mule scatter about in this field with the change of a light colored field turning into a black field as those teams plow and roll over the dirt. The pitcher is so beautiful. No wonder peoples traveling down 289 (Preston Road) would stop day in and day out to take pitcher of ten team turning a old field into a new one.

Hunting Wild Animals

Mother would ask which way are you going? Don't go off and stay till dark, and stay out of them thick woods.

This brought up the question of where I was to go hunting. They ask me had I ever been hunting in the wooded bottom west of the Shepton School and Church. I tell them no lie. I said yes. And they were furious and told me I was never never to go beyond the school hunting. I ask why and said I can all way kill some rabbit down there, referring to, as they call it, the bottom or the Jungle Bottom. Dad said that place was so thick you could get lost or tangle up in the thick brush and could not find your way out. He told me that it had wofes, black bear, bob cat and black panther and God knows what else. This was back in the thirties and the bottom was a untame jungle. They said that even deer had venture in there also.

The creek which was name White Rock Creek started far up north of us and run along Preston Road criss crossing Preston some place as far as a cupple of miles one side east or west of Preston and run down into Trinity River. In some place along White Rock Creek the wood was like a jungle and in some places still is. I remember men use to come by the little road behind the school and rock pit going down in the bottom to trap and hunt. I also remember that we were taught in school not to go down that road by one self. The teacher would take us on a field trip down that road but never over a hundred yards. Even in the brightest part of the day the further you go down that road the darker it got.

It was in the late thirties a dress up man came to our house and talk to Dad about cleaning some of the bottom out. It was some Doctor out of upstate or Dallas. Anyway Dad told him if he could get some help he would. He told Dad he would pay him for his work and the others. During the winter month whin work was lay by on the farm Dad got Uncle Ronney and Tank and some time Mr. Hen to help. I remember very well whin they first went down there they were really scared. Even the team of horses were skiddish so automatic that made Dad and them some what scared. They had never hunt that part of the bottom. It was dark and dreary during winter month and Dad and them would go carrying the dogs and guns, saws, ax, karseen, plenty of matches. First they would secure the team of horse, build a fire and began thinning out brush. There were one thing they did. There would be one of them stood guard with shot gun ready while the other two or three work. I would stand around the fire keeping it burning as they begin to inch back through the thicket cutting, trimming and stacking wood. Brought out a wagon load every day, and once a month they would hall to town the wood they got and sell it.

The Doctor came out one day and lay out a plan of what he wanted. Also brought out barb wire and gate fence post. He wanted enough land cleared to build a small barn and a fence in place to put some horses. He paid them and I my self don't even remember seeing him again but as they clean the land they began to build the fence. And I suppose he told Dad when ther money would be there and it was. Every week or so or a month the can nailed to the fence post had some money in it. I don't no how much but they all seem happy about it. Plus they got the wood free, kill some big swamp rabbit, squirrel, and possum.

I don't no what happen but they laid out a few day. If I can recall they had see some thing they did not like. I think they said it was a panther, a big black long tail. They had all way seen the bob cat, and had kill one and got a bounty for it. Whin looking at a movie of the jungle and swamp that is what that place remind you of. They could have said Big Foot live down there and people would have beleave it. I do no that they had track some prisoners up through there because they had the state police come by our house and ask and warn us about the excape prisoners. That within itself was frighten especial to Dad and them others.

Dad then clear bottom land during winter and rainy days for three or four year. They got the first cupple acres cleared and a fence around it and the Doctor brought four horses out there and stack hay outside the fence and "Horse and Mule Feed." Dad would go feed them, and sometime send me to feed them.

I all way like to go down there to feed them. I would take my gun and kill me a rabbit or two. As time roll on more and more hunter and horse back rider began to venture back down that little trail or road. It finally come to the creek and I think Dad and them was a bit suprise to see that there were a old bridge across the White Rock Creek. Also a fording place. I suppose it had been there for years but had not been use.

Dust Storms and Blue Whislers

Whin the dust storms roared across the north of us in Collin County we were face with another problum. The time would usual be late fall whin the last of the cotton was being scrap pick by the old women and children, while the old men would drive those horses and mules huffing and puffing up and down the field plowing the black earth. They were laying the plowed ground by for the winter before the rain and snow came while the women were dumping ther sacks of cotton. It seem that all would wind up at the wagon the same time whether they had a full sack or not. The men with those teams of puffing tired horses would some how slow down enough to all meet on an end, walk over in a huddle, roll a smoke, take a chew of tabacco.

Being a boy between seven and ten, these are the words I remember hearing come out of those huddle of men and women. While all would look to the north and north west, men would say, Look like we're in for it. The women would say, Child, I show hate to see them kind of storms come through. No telling what you get out of this one. Look yonder, girl, you see that red in or on the top of that blue. You no what that mean. We gonner get a good storm with dis here cold spell.

One of the older women who had been around longer and was more wiser would say, Cold spell. Shit. Dat look like one of dem blue whisler. She call the blue norther a blue whisler because it whisle through the cracks of the old house and make them sing. Some one would say, Oh, my, God. We better get to de house so me and dem chillen can start nailing up tin to dem window and try to chink up some of dem hole. Child, you no how bad that sand storm can be along with that blue whisler. The last time we had one I forgot to put the top on the flour can and we ate sand for the longest. We better go. Another say,

Look yonder, girl, you see that red in or on top of that blue.
You no what that mean. We gonner get a good storm
with dis here cold spell.

Don't forget to screw the top on all your food. I hate this sand storm cause that make me have to wash all most twice this week. All that sand get in your clothes and bed. Its trouble, child. Somebody else say, Better off than some sister so and so, ain't hardly got no window in they house and she said that they can't get that white man to put none in. Last word said would be, I'll be praying for you all. Somebody say, Me too. We'll see you Sunday at church if the Lord willing and the creek don't rise. Come on kid. Let hurry home and get them hole stuff up and you kid get in enough wood for tonite.

Now that is what and how the women did whin the storm come. It wouldn't be right to leave out the story of how the men would react. The men just about finish ther smoke and chaw, whin one would say, Man we better head for the barn. Look like a blue whisler headen this way and look like it pushing a sand storm in front of it. Boy, the way it look, it will be here in a cupple of hours.

Here is one case of helping each other. This field where the men and my Dad were working was across the creek and past the barn so Dad was right at home. The other two men was my Uncle Ronney and my cousin Fat or Tank, whatever you wish to call him. Any way Dad would tell them, You all got longer way to home than I do, so take a wagon and head home. You no you got to go milk, gather egg, feed the stock for Ray. I'll take the other teams to the barn and take care of them and get all the stock bed down. That mean he had to unharness the horses, feed and lock them up, feed the hog if I had not fed them. Usually I fed every day but with the storm coming we would feed extra and shut up the chickens, chop wood and get it in.

Ruth and Mom was chinking holes. This is one time Mom would say to Bessie Lee, Girl, get you little butt out there with Jr. and get some chips in so you can stay out of my way.

Anyway by the time Dad would get through, the storm would hit—wind and sand first. Some time the sand was so thick you could hardly see. So much sand would come through it would stack up side of the house and fence row like snow. The next thing some few hours later, it was time to get the drip bucket and tub ready to catch water or snow coming in the house.

Let me remind you it was not just in winter time. These storm would also come in early spring. We would get the same kind of storm only they would be worse on the young cotton and corn crop. The sand storm would chop, slice and cover the crop. We use to get a lot of hail in the spring of the year and lose the wheat crop which was about to head out into grain. The cotton and corn could be planted over, but part of the grain would be lost for that year.

Beside the lost of crop whin the blue whisler came along with the sand storm, the sand were as good as a sand blasting of the type use in shop these days. As disastrous as it may seem, those sand storm created jobs. After the storm, paint jobs were needed. Just like the well diggers during the drought come by to find water, paint crews travel through the county looking to paint houses and barns. You had to paint, or barn and house would dry rot or eventual the sand and wind would beat it to the ground.

By the grace of God one thing about the sand storm, it help the farm ground. This is black land country and I don't think I have to tell any one about the sticky, black mud whin it get wet. Whin the sand storm come through, it left a thin layer of sand on top of the black soil. Whin this was turn under and mix with the black soil, it loosen it enough that a field that was not rocky would plow up easy without sticking, and whin you plant seed in it the seed had breathing room to pop out of the ground faster.

But with the ground a little loose, more rocks turn up in a

already rocky field. So before planting time and after harvest of all crops, whin the land was laid by for the winter, women and children were able to go in to the rocky fields, pick up rock, and load them on a wagon. And the farmer would use the rocks to plug up drains and washed out ditches, which was ther form of land conservation. The rocks were use for mud road, ditch crossing, tamping around fence post, decoration of yard and making up of lime and water for a white wash paint. Picking up rock was another way for a famley to earn a little extra money from land owner.

There could be a sand storm or a blue norther or both together which was the worst. One thing for sure, if you ever look to the north and see red over blue, head for cover. The red was the sand from the west; the blue was the wind that boiled up the sand and it looked like the red sand was riding on the winds. This was the sand storm and blue norther combined. You ain't never been whip till you get a sand whipping.

Farming

One of the most beautiful thing I love about the farming was just about every part of the world I visit during the late forties and fifties, even some part of the world I saw in the sixties, the peoples were still using hand tool, ox and horses to work ther land. And that brought back my remember of those days of how we did our farming.

The large farm owner had lot of land any where from 200–300 acre or more. But only a portion were cleared enough for crops. During the winter men would clear trees. The bord'arc wood were hard and were use for house block, fence post and barn upright support. The farm worker used the soft wood for fire wood and halled it to Plano, sold it to make ends meet. In that way they could buy flour, sugar, garden seeds etc. Another thing, by more land being cleared it would mean more for the share cropper to have. Another good thing about it, the new land would produce great amount of crops. As the years pass on more land was cleared. Better crops were made. A lot of land was clear during the drought. I used to help saw the trees, stack wood into cords and drag bord'arc post and stack them.

I guess this is one reason I came back to the farm after growing up on the farm, clearing wood, tilling the rich soil and working the seed into the ground, watching them sprout through the earth. I don't think there is nothing no more beautiful than watching a seed sprout, even with all the sweat that you put into the plants from working the tough ground to a soft smooth carpet like field. Even with the bloody hand that you would get from pulling the sharp blades of Johnson grass except a spot here and there that you would flat crop and dehead the grass and sack the tops. That mean you would cut the seeded heads of the grass, then chop and dig the grass up by the roots. That what you call flat chopping or flat weeding.

One of the most beautiful thing I love about the farming was just about every part of the world I saw in the sixties, the peoples were still using hand tool, ox and horses. And that brought back my remember of those days of how we did our farming.

Once you had chop and thin the rows of cotton or corn, it would out grow the grass. All you had to do is watch the beautiful growth until harvest.

This mean not only bloody fingers from the sharp burrs, but blister and bloody knees from crawling on the hot soft ground. Sometime knees slipping in dry crack, skin the side of the knees and legs. Even the bare toes would be blister from the hot dirt while on your knees to rest a tired aching back. Sometime no shoes or the toe worn out.

But all in all we made it. After all the harvest was over women would have time to go fishing and play or visit each other, some time getting up early in the morning, get dinner ready, and walk for three or four miles to visit. Whin the women would get together you could hear thing like this. Child, I'm so glad all that cotton is out. I had to work like the dickens this year. And I'm show gonner enjoy this time of year and make my self a treat with the little extry money I made. This is one time I gonner get my self some new shoes and enough cloth to make me some thing decent to wear to church. It was hard work, but we made a good crop this year.

These was the good years in the late thirties after the dust and sand storms and coming out of the Depression. I remember Dad and my uncle and other men sitting around talking about how good the crops was this year. Dad would say, I guess Ray made some more this year. We went down to the mule barn last week. Ray bought two or three working mules and we breeded four mares. He said something about he might get a tractor. Some one would say, Is that right? Then my Uncle Ronney said, I don't care how many datburn tractor he get, I ain't gonner drive one of dem thing. I'll stick to my team.

Well, I can tell you this. As long as I can remember while Uncle Ronney was with Ray he did not drive a tractor. He move to Clint Haggard about the same time I and my famley left Ray. I visit Uncle Ronney in the middle fifties and he was still plowing with a team of mule. Any way Ray got the tractor and Dad was the only one drove the tractor, an Iron Lug Wheel Farmal. Dad learn me how to drive it and all summer I would brake ground with it.

The house work, yard work and garden work were left to the women and children, black or white. Also the chopping of the grassy field. While chopping, there may be one old man to keep the hoe sharp. Kid who hall the water was call the water boy. There used to be a song the worker sing about the water boy.

Hey, Water Boy
Where is dat water?
I'm so thirsty I can cry.
If you dont hurry Water Boy,
I may die.

Dad would plow the garden real good, completely pulverizing it to a smooth silky like ground. But no men I no of work the garden except to cover and dig the Irish potatoes with the team of mule and with a one man middle buster. Mom would all way open up the garden rows or punch holes in the ground for the seed, and would all way let me put the seed out. She said kids had a growing hand and she would show us kid how to put seed out. Ruth was very good. Sometimes I put too many out. Mom would give Bessie Lee one or two seed. She would tell Bessie Lee, Girl, you get over yonder and set down somewhere. I ain't got no seed to waste.

Once the seed was up we keep the weeds and grass out the same way we did cotton and corn. And whin the garden were ready to harvest, as I said before, Mom would say, Tomorrow is garden day. Got to pick beans. So you kid got to get a good night sleep. Next morning after breakfast and some time before breakfast, off to the garden we go. Mom fix Dad coffee and breakfast. We all got our little bucket and go. Once we got the garden food gather, we usual wash it at the creek by the well and spring on our way back to the house. Then start shelling bean for canning purpose.

This was still the years before the forties and the garden crops were just as good as the field. In fact most time the garden were better because we took great care of each plant. There is nothing as beautiful as planting a seed, then watch it pop out of the ground—a sprig, to the first two leave, to the bush, to the bud, to the bloom, to the fruit. The harvest part is gathering and preserving, cooking it to taste. The easy part is placing it on the table and eating it. That mean smacking down on a spoon full of fresh green bean and potatoes and licking your chops. Every time I think of the plant growing from seed to fruit, I think it is as beautiful as the birth of a baby and watching it grow to a successful young man or woman.

Fear of Failure

Reader, if you recall, I've told you that we move from Ray Haggard farm to Allen, and after about a year and a half we move back.

I'm at my sister Ruth home here in the outskirts of Edgewood on her small farm. Its 1:00 A.M., and we just had a long talk about why we move, the hope and prospect we had after we move, and the disaster we fell into whin we move back where we left from.

Dad had been with Ray Haggard since he was twelve. In the early 1940s peoples began to get better jobs moving to town. Mule and horse field work were being replaced by tractor. All the share crops earnings were use to pay back borrow money, and I suppose Dad look around and seen what was out side of his perimeters and realize, I got a famley to take care of and year after year I ain't got a penny, after the year of no borrowing money.

I can remember the sight on his face when he first tell us we moving—one that I'd never seen before. There were a sign of happiness in his slow gracious movement, the shy smile on his face, more like a grin, then a laugh. As he walk in the house, I heard him say, Millie, you and the kid come in here. I got some thing to tell you. Mom a little slow coming to the big famley room, thinking all the time, Some thing had bad happen.

I think the reason mom acted like that was because dad never was a talker, but whin he did talk, he got the attention of any body around him. As we gather in this room Dad look around at Mom, me, Ruth, and Bessie Lee, and a smile came on his lip. And he said, How would you all like to move?

All of us, all most at the same time, Where? Where? Where? To town? To Plano?

Dad answer, Nope. Allen, Texas.

All us said, Whin? Whin? Whin?

Probly in a week or two.

Somewhere in the back of my mind I can hear these words from Mr. Ray before we left, Pete, how in the world are you going to make it? If you got to go I won't stop you. I don't imagine you going to make it, but you can come on back whin you get ready.

We got to move all right and thing were better than they had ever been. The place we move was own by Lavon Dairy. It was east of Allen, around 250 acre. Dad was in charge of the dairy. All we had to do was work the farm and plant what ever we please and the profit was our. We had a nice home, hog, and chickin. I was raising pigeon. For a black famley we had every thing with nothing hold against, two car, and money. By the time cotton was ready and the corn were making a possible eighty to a hundred bushel per acre, my dad move us back to Ray Haggard. No more share cropping, just a farm hand. Very upsetting for mother and us three kids.

The question then, is what happen and why we had to move back. Well, I or any one could speculate on a number of thing, but I can tell you for sure. After being in a place for as many years as my dad had been, the way he started out as a farmer as a kid and always with the same man, on his own and unable to read or write, I think it was more of a psychological effect, after moving from one inviroment you no so well, to a better inviroment. But still theres a question of it being secure enough to take care of a famley. So here you get afraid some time. Dad had gold platter in hand and silver spoon in mouth. His new boss want him to stay, but there was fear. Dad knew he had at least a place to go back to but didn't know for how long. All ready our house was taken and every body had stop share cropping and twelve acres was gone. But there was a

My dad move us back to Ray Haggard. No more share cropping, just a
farm hand. Very upsetting for mother and us three kids.

little small house not even big enough for the famley.

Once again I watch Dad drive up, get out of the car, come in
the house, a little angry and a little sad. No smile this time but
more of a frighten look on his face, as if some one had said, I
told you you couldn't make it out there.

So whin he call out, All you come in here. Let me tell you
what we going to do.

Mom: What Eddie?

Us three kid: What Dad?

Dad: Well, we is going to move.

Everybody: Where? Where?

Dad: Back to Ray Haggard.

Mom: What?

Ruth: I don't want to move.

Bessie Lee: What for?

Me: I lacked one more day laying the corn by. You mean to tell me I did all this work for nothing?

Mom: Eddie, Can't you find some where else to move beside back where we left from?

But in a few days we move back to the same inviroment, only with worse condition. Famley split because the only house then available was too small. I move in with Aunt Emma and her nephew Tank. No more share cropping, only day to day wages. Thing were never the same. Fear had taken charge of Dad life, and poverty took over his famley. Thing didn't get any better in a year or two. Dad trying to gain self control of anger and fear. We move again. In a year we move again and Dad overcome fear after getting another job beside farm life. First time he have some money in his pocket and other thing start to have more meaning than famley. Every body began to look after ther own self. Although love and care for each other still exist, anger and fear has a way of up setting and turning things around and around and even up side down. But slowly we did crawl out of it. We made it by the help of God and strong famley ties. Tough time never last, but tough people all way do. I wrote a poem about tough time.

Tough time never last.
Life is sweet. Life is swell.
You can look up. You can look down.
Still, there is nothin to be found.
You can look left. You can look right.
And thing seems out of site.
We no that tomorrow is not promis.
But we dont have to live in sorror.
Don't look back because you wont fine any tracks.
Look ahead. You ain't dead.

What Kept Us Going

It strange to look back in the past whin work were all sweat and muscles. Every job were strait from the body muscles. Some of the work strain every vein in your body. Even tears roll out of one eyes. I can remember men and women say, She or he work ther poor soul to death.

Now that I've been through some of that blood and sweat for a living, I understand why they said this. I been one of any where from ten to twenty peoples out in a field chopping cotton with grass as thick as hair on a dog back. Some time bending down for hours pulling grass from around cotton you could hardly see for weeds, with a row a mile long and take all day, some time two day, to chop one row.

It would been nice, chopping the cotton, if not for the ups and downs. The cotton were so bad that every time you make one whack with your hoe you had to bend over to pull the grass from around the cotton. It was like bending over doing three whack down to one whack standing. One would think in grassy cotton like this you would never get from one end to the other, the rows being one mile long. By the time you get to the top of the hill and a half day gone you look down the row and say, Lord have mercy. I still got a half mile to go.

The older peoples probly start thinking about I've got to work all the week five and a half days or six and only make a dollar a day, five or six dollar a week, and half of it go to the boss man to pay back what you had borrow that winter so you could eat and feed your famley. On top of all that you probly had to buy medicine or pay a doctor.

You think, these days of the push button world, How in the world did they make it? I can tell you how they made it. First thing they did at night, they read the Bible and pray. The next morning the first thing they did whin ther feet hit the floor,

You think, these days of the push button world, How did
they make it? I can tell you. First thing they did at night,
they read the Bible and pray.

they went on ther knees and thank God for another day and
say, Lord help me make it through this day.

And one of the beautiful sound in the heat of the day whin
the blister bust in your hand from chopping and the blood
running from your hand where the tough Johnson grass blade
have cut your hand, back hurting from bending, foot hurting
from standing, clothes sweaty and sticky, then a tear began to

roll from your eyes, some body would raise up, pull the bonnet off, wipe the tear and sweat, look up at the sun beaming down at about 100 degree and say, Lord help me make it the rest of this day, and start to hum mum mum mum, then every body brake out with a humming song, like "Nobody Knows the Trouble I See," "Swang Low Sweet Chariot," "I'm Going Home on the Morning Train," and "I've Got a Home Over in Glory, Just Wait and See."

These type of song would be like cool breeze blowing in your face, dry up the sweat and tear, rough up the hand. Seem like the hoe get sharp, strength get in your back, feet get happy, grass get tender and you could see the cotton sticking up through the grass. You get to feeling so good that you pay no mind at the time or look at the sun to know the hour. Then all of a sudden some one would say, Thank you Jesus. I've made this day.

Some one else would say, Child, another day and another dollar.

Some body else would say, Yeh, child, but look where it going.

Where was it going? Well look at it this way. Fifty cent to the boss, twenty-five cent for snuff or tobacco and fifteen cent for food. Well, let head for the shack. Got to stir up a little supper. Probly left over bean, fry some potatoes, make some corn bread or biscus.

Most of the time kid who were old enough would be sent home to start the fire. Whin I start cooking at seven, mother would put out enough of bean to cook for dinner and supper, corn meal too. On that note every body throw ther hoe over ther shoulder and head to the shanty with a good night and, I'll see you tomorrow if the Lord willing and the creek don't rise. By By.

104

Run for Cover

I don't remember the exact way to make home brew, which is a beer. The only ingredients I remember were yeast, mash, and water. Put in a crock and let it set for a number of days before you bottle and cap it. The longer it cure the stronger it get. My baby sister and I would steal us a drink of it from time to time. Ruth would smell it and then go tell it.

I don't think I will ever forget the time I got drunk. During the raining cold days whin we were not clearing and cleaning up bottom and fence row, cutting or chopping wood, we would hunt and gather scrap iron. At one time or nother during winter month we would hall it to Dallas and sell pig iron or what you call short iron. Would bring pretty good money and the money come in handy in winter.

My cousin and Dad drink beer. My uncle drink any thing we make. My uncle bought a gallon of wine that was called Sweet Lucy. On our way back home my Dad told me I could have a sip, but my uncle keep giving me sips. By the time we got back to the house I could not walk. Some one put me to bed. For three day I could not get up. I vomit and mess my bed up. Mother would clean and change bed and keep praying. In three days I came to my senses and whin I did my mother were standing over the bed and look down on me and said, Don't you feel ashame of your self?

I felt so bad about the whole thing I could not say any thing. I felt like crawling in a hole. I no my mother was very concern about me. I think I was about twenty year old before I drink anything else to excess. I never got that drunk again but have had some good feeling.

In 1950–52 during my station in New Orleans there was not much to do but play penny poker and drink. One pay day I lost all my money and could not buy no wine. I sober up and take a shower. I smell my skin and it stunk like wine. And to this day I've never drunk any more wine ever. During all the years I drink enough to build a lake but no wine and very little beer. Only whiskey and vodka. And I haven't taken a drink of that since 1986, nor do I smoke. I do chew a little.

Boot legging was common in my growing up days. And all most every body made ther own beer during the thirties and part of forties. Some people made it to sell. Others made it for home use. My Dad made brew for home and people who would visit. He also peddled it on a small scale. Every time he left home he would put a few bottles in the trunk of his car or under the back seat.

Most of the real boot leggers had some kind of juke joint. They made whiskey and beer or go to Dallas and buy it to sell, and they got away pretty good. They would pay off the law or keep a look out who let them know whin there were a raid so they had time to hide it. Whin the state police or the county sheriff begin to crack down, they did a lot of house to house searching. Mr. Ray would all way let his farm famleys no whin the police were coming.

Mr. Ray say to my dad, Pete, you got any booze down ther you got to get rid of it. They going to do some house to house search in a day or so. My dad would gather up his beer and beer making material and hide it up the branch. Ray also tell my cousin, Fat, you'd better stay home Saturday night. They going to raid that joint. Then Tank would say to me, June, I guess we better go some place else Saturday. Frisco is going to be too hot with the Good Old Boys.

We call the police the Good Old Boys or the Do Right Boys. But whin we be in the field along Hiway 289 and see the state troopers go by in ther black and white car, some body would say, Ther go the Skonk or Pole Cat. I think the Good Old Boys get ther name because on one Saturday or Friday night they would go by the juke joint and be just like every body else playing the juke box and wouldn't say a word about the drinking or gambling, and the next week night come by and hall you off to jail. This was whin the Skonk and Good Old Boys turn up together and be mean as hell, scaring, punching and swanging that billie club, herding you into the cattle trailer.

There were a lot of women in boot legging. This one woman sold food and whiskey. The people would drive up to her house, hold up ther finger to indicate how many bottle of liquer they want. No word were never pass, only hello, goodby. This lady had a husband who love to gamble, spend every penny he got his hand on. So he would steal his wife whiskey and sell it. He would stand outside the house and wait until some one would drive up, hold up ther hand, collect the money, go across the street, and gamble it away. The wife would get angry, cuss him out and keep telling him, I'm going to brake you up from stealing my whiskey. He pay no attention.

Word got out that she was going to stop this mess. One day she was frying chickin. Some one come for a bottle. The husband went in the house for the whiskey and started out. His wife slap him upside the head with a frying pan of hot grease and chickin. He broke the front door and screen door down and had a chickin leg stuck upside his head. Almost kill him. And he had the mark for the rest of his life.

That just one type of thing that would happen between a husband and wife. Thing were never too good whin ther were whiskey and gambling. Whin I use to go to the juke joint I watch the way the bottles were deliver under cover by women and men. You could tell most men boot legger. They all way wore ducking over alls and a coat too big. The boot legger would buy a quart or half gallon; a quart cost $5. He would break it down into half pints, which were most popular size, and sell for $2.50 or $3. That were good money. So whin they

107

were caught and hauled off to jail and the magistrate told them their fine, they would reach in there pocket and pull out a roll of bills, pay their fine and walk out the door. An hour later they back in business.

Back to boot legging. Whin my dad was making booze there were all way some body dropping by to buy a few bottle of beer. He would also take booze with him on week end and to parties every week. He did not keep too much. Whin ever Ray would get word that the sheriff was going to make a check or raid Dad would take his booze some place safe. The big scale boot legger were able to pay off some body and never got caught. Those who did get caught paid ther fine and the next day went and got a new supply.

I remember the juke joint in Frisco. They keep plenty of whiskey and booze and a man or two to look out for the police. If word came the police were coming, the owner would take his booze down in a special place in the corn field. The police and sheriff department were pretty smart. They would show up on a Friday or Saturday. By the way, these places open only on weekend and holidays, but you could all way buy a drink. Now back to the police. As I said, on Friday and Saturday the police would show up and watch the dancing, put nickle in the juke box or the other name for it was the picklelow machine. Some time one of the women of the night would grab one of the police and tell him, Man you sure look good and drag him out on the floor. However, they would refuse, at least in public.

This would go on for a few week. Then on a good work week and all the cotton picker in town, plenty of money and booze, the police would show up like they all way did with a bus and cattle truck and act like they all way did, but about 10:30 or 11:00 thing change. Police would pop up every where and surround the place. The next thing they would have every body line up collecting gun, knife, straight razor. A lot of women carried straight razor and could whip it out of ther bosum as fast as a snake could strike and cut you so fast, make you look like shredded cheese. Any way, here come the truck and cattle wagon, load up every body in and around the place and hall them to McKinney Jail. All who could pay there way out did. The rest had to stay in jail. If you were a good worker the boss would get you out of jail. If you did sorry work you stay in jail and work your way out. During this time the county had work farms, like pea patch, onion patch; road work; rock piles where you busted rock into gravel for building roads. There were farms, wooded area and road side to be cleared and clean up. Pea patch was field where you plant, chop and harvest. All who couldn't pay ther way out and them that the boss did not want back on ther farm went to the pea patch.

One of the most talk about thing and some of the memory I have about the bootlegging and gambling house were the site of police, or word come that the fuzz is coming. The fuzz is known as cop. Soon as the word "cops" come, man, niggers would grab the money and dice and scatter. Jumping out of window, two or three trying to get out the door the same time. Boy, they would be running for cover like a rabbit running for the briar patch whin a dog show up. Ever body would not get away. Those who did, the next week whin they see each other, one would say, Man, did you get away?

Yeah, man! Did you?

You better no I got away! I ain't ready to go to that pea patch. No way in Hell they were going to catch me once I got out that door.

In some way I associate boot legging and gambling as part of each other because both are illegal, especial during the time I grew up. I witness and look on a lot of diffrent way to gamble. I tryed my hand at dice, card betting, or games like pitching pennies. That was during my army days.

My dad was a boot legger and a gambler. First time I knew this is the gray hound rabbit hunt. There was a number of city and country men had gray hound, and they would breed them just for racing. There use to be a lot of open space and plenty of Jack Rabbit. The fastest of this rabbit were the Blue Side Jack Rabbit. Every week end in the late fall and winter men would gather in a big field, preferble one with no fence. They would chain hold ther dog and walk through a field until they see a rabbit sitting or jump up. The rabbit would jump up and whin it get 50 or 100 yard away some one would say, Turn the dogs aloose. And the men would unsnap the chain and off they go.

The bet would all ready be on. Those who had money would bet pretty good money on their dog. Those who did not have money would put up a bet with beer, whiskey, a puppy out of the winners dog, gun, knife, hog, chickin, just about any thing they had to bet. Probly those who were professional gambler, who did it for a living, would even bet ther wife or girl friend. Even back then the die hard gambler had two or three women working for them as business associate. These women would take care of selling the booze, cook and sell dinner, and sell ther body.

The next open range betting was chickin fights. My Dad raise chickin. Each had ther own little pens. He would never fight his own with each other, but each week they would meet at some one house or a desenated spot where they think the police would not find them and have chickin fight. They would bet on the chickin before the fight. They would hold them in ther arms and have a blindfold on them. Whin the blind was pull off, they tease each other, making the chickin mad by poking each at the other. Whin the chickin was steam up enough, the men would drop them on the ground and the chickin would fight until one would run or get kill.

There were some pretty prominent peoples who had

fighting chickin. Some chickin even import from Mexico. Regular yard chickin were also use. The big yard rooster against the small game cock to train the game cock. The egg of the game chickin were expensive, maby one dollar each egg to probly five dollar. You could also order eggs or baby chick for setting or train the young. My dad bought chickin. I don't no how much he paid, but anywhere from twenty-five dollar to who knows. I know these days those who raise fighting cock will go as high as a $1000 dollar or more. I've heard that those who is in the business travel a lot just to fight chickin. My dad finely sold all his fighting cocks.

On to the next gambling game. Shooting dice and playing card I guess have cause more hungry famleys and more cutting and shooting as any gambling in the world, especial in the Black Race. Crooked dice slip into a game or card dealer dealing from the bottom, or card put up ther coat sleeve. I've seen gamblers on Friday or Saturday get paid and don't go home, pay a bill, or even buy a loaf of bread. And would not have a potato in the house. And house full of hungry kids.

These poor souls who were sweating and losing their money the most, knowing they was about broke, you could hear them say thing like this:

"Come on Baby 7, make 11."

"I need this point bad as a dead man need a coffin."

"Come on 11, kid need some shoes, Momma need some drawers."

"Snake eyes man, you crap out."

Back home kids would sing song, "Momma in the kitchin cooking rice. Daddy round the corner shooting dice."

Usually the places where the games were played there were all way boot leg whiskey. People who gambles usually drink and the professional gambler knows this and would feed the weak gambler this booze just to beat him out of his money. The

I've seen gamblers on Friday or Saturday get paid and don't go home,
pay a bill, or even buy a loaf of bread. And would not have a
potato in the house.

gambler was something to look at if you were like me. The
gamblers all way fasinate me as a boy because I wonder where
they would get all that money all around the table. Of course,
the money would all way wind up in two or three men hand.

I been in places whin I was a kid whin a fight brake out, a
gun shooting, a knife cutting, getting tromp on trying to get out
of the way. In Dallas down on Elm Street, in Plano and Frisco
and some houses in the country, I remember at least once a
week as a kid we would meet at another famley house for card

games. Some would play cards "for drink or smell." The two who win the game got to drink whiskey, the two looser get a smell. All way whiskey. Some would play dominoes, some shooting dice, most of the time for money. It may not be much—penny and nickle games.

There were all way some one to play the turn table victrola record player, or some one to pick a gitar and play the harp. There were one man from Plano would all way go where the party was with his gitar, and white and black saddle shoes for tap dancing, just to pick up a few penny. He was good. He sing and play the harp and gitar. He would teach kid to tap. Any where the kids see him they would beg him to teach them to dance. He would stay a while, because he was all way on the move walking just about every where he go. He was a stepper; he could really walk.

One thing while growing up, my peoples, the Blacks, did not have to have a whole lot of instrument to get rhythm whether it be blues or church songs. Some time those who had any music ability would get together with banjo, gitar, wash board, tub for drum and harp. I look at some of the dances today and I've seen those dances whin I was a kid. This brake dance they got now and the funkey dance, I did this whin I was a kid. The funkey roll was a down home blues record or it was call "Put Me in the All Music." The brake dance today, getting on the floor or the back and spinning around, this dance whin I was a kid was call getting down. They would do the split, get on ther knees and the stomic, on the back and do all kind of butt twisting and rolling.

There were some other dances. They were call the Hen Peck. Two peoples stand in front of each other and work right on down to the floor on ther knees and then back up again. And they would peck at each other with ther neck, just like chickin, stand and peck at each other, one side to the other and face to face in the same rhythm, like the men hold the chickins priming them for the fight.

Some of the other dances were doing the shimmy, same as shake rattle and roll, shake it to the east, shake it to the west, shake it to the one you love the best. By doing this on a dance floor you could tell pretty well who was going with who. Then there was the turkey hop, two people on the floor hopping round like a chickin with ther head cut off. A lot of time there were fight, whin a woman or man dance with some body else more than ther husband or wife or girl friend or boy friend.

My mother use to show us how to do the Charleston. She were very lite footed.

Jack Rabbit

There are diffrent kind of rabbit—cotton tail and swamp rabbit, which is a bit bigger than a cotton tail and live close to the water and wet swamp area, and are very tricky.

Every body knows about the tame white rabbit and the Peter Cotton Tail. But there is the open range Jack Rabbit with the long, long ears and legs. There are two kind that I know. I remember what the men would say about the Jack Rabbit whin they would run the gray hounds. The distinction between the Blue Side and the other Jack Rabbit is the blue side and the way they run once the Blue Side get up from his bed. They hop along on three leg as if they will tease the dogs. Once the dogs get close to it, it is like a car whin you mash the gas peddle, it get over drive. The Blue Side will drop that forth leg. And some one in the crowd would say, That a Blue Side and he is going to be Hell to catch. And it would.

The dog with the longest wind was the only one to catch it or run until the dog fall out or give up. Those who know ther dog and ther strength some time would not let them run. Some time the men, as long as the dog run, they would keep betting that the dog will catch the rabbit. Some time they would. Some time they would not. The dog give up but the rabbit do not. It just look back and smile, as if to say, Goodby, see you later alagater. You'll never get your chop on me.

The Blue Side rabbit hop along on three leg as if they will tease
the dog. Once the dog get close to it, it will drop that forth leg.
And some one in the crowd would say, that a Blue Side and he
going to be Hell to catch.

Fill Up on the Holy Spirit

We were taught the Bible at home. Just about every day or night we had time to study the scripture with Mother. My dad did not read. We had to read and learn certain scripture of the Bible and one thing for sure, Bessie Lee would be still during this period. We never sit down at the table one by one. We sit down and eat together and not before prayer and thank God for the food. And we did not go to bed before we said our prayer. We were taught them from the time we could talk. Our first prayer:

My Lord lay me down to sleep
If I die before I wake
I pray to the Lord my soul to take
Bless Momma and Daddy
Bless Ruth and Bessie Lee
Bless Every Body
Amen

Going to church has all way been the back bone support for the Black people. Meeting people at church, having fun at church. Most all the farm community would be there at church on Sundays and Wednesdays. And above all Black folk felt better going to church after chopping cotton all week.

Every time the church door open we were there: Sunday School, Church, and Pray Meeting every Wednesday night and any other function. Wednesday night pray meeting was said to be like a car. You have to stop and fill up the car with gas every once in a while. So on Wednesday night you go to pray meeting. You pray, sing, and fill up on the Holy Spirit so it will last until Sunday. There were a lot of Wednesday that men could not be there due to ther work schedule, especial during harvest time.

The thing I remember about church as a kid growing up, my mother were teaching me Bible. She also taught Sunday School. I remember once the devotional part of Sunday School was over, kid and adult broke down in age groups and moved off to one corner or the other with ther teacher for this Sunday lesson. About forty-five minutes later we reassemble for dismissal.

Kid learn how to read in Sunday School. There were even grown peoples learn to read out of ther Bibles at Sunday School and pray meeting. There were Sunday School every Sunday morning. There were church just about all day, and sometime even on the Sunday night, especial on Church Anniversary and Home Coming and closing out a Revival.

There were only one Baptisement a year, no matter how many join church. We would go to church this Sunday. After church you would go home, get your food, and head out to Doctor Dyes for dinner by the creek. Dinner on the ground were all way great. There were all way plenty of food—chickin, red bean, black peas, green bean with potatoes, potato salad, greens, dressing and gravy, and plenty of cake, pies, cookies, and hand made ice cream.

After dinner we had service and line up for the dip in the water. While the preacher dip you, the women would line the banks singing song. After all the baptising, kid would play, people would sit around and talk until some one would say, Well, I guess I better get home and feed and milk that white man cows.

I better go too, I got to chop that old woman some wood for next week if I want something to eat. This is what a husband would say.

I'll see you Wednesday at pray meeting if the Lord is willing and the creek don't rise. And on this note parent start gathering up kid and all say, Good by. See you later.

There were only one Baptisement a year, no matter how many join the church. After church you would go home, get your food, and head out to Doctor Dyes for dinner by the creek.

The only preacher I remember real well was a woman, Sister Riddle, in her long black robe (sometime white robe on special occasion) and big white hankchief throwed over her shoulder for wiping sweat. Whin I was young going to church, Sister Riddle favorite songs before she started to preach was "I'm Going to Lay Down My Burden" and "Down By the Riverside."

I love good singing and I love to sing with male chorus and choirs. I can't sing but I try to. It nothing like sitting back and hearing an old Negro spiritual or an old sister or deacon lead a old 100 hymn. (A old 100 hymn was from slave times—deeply felt and with a spiritual feeling, such as "Guide Me O Thou

Great Jehovah," "I Love the Lord," "He Heared My Cry," "Walk With Me," "Amazing Grace," and "Steal Away.")

Some time now day or night I can hear my mother singing. She use to sing all the time around the house, especial whin she was tired or worried about something. Song like "Just a Closer Walk With Thee," "Jesus Keep Me Near the Cross," "I'm Going to Lay Down My Burden," and "Down By the Riverside." I like the song "If I Could Hear My Mother Pray Again," "I Love the Lord, He Hear My Cry," "I Will Trust in the Lord," "Mothers Bow," and "Precious Lord."

Churches these days have gotten away from most of the old spiritual singing. Choirs with all type of musical instruments has dominated the singing. Some drowns out words. Don't get me wrong. The music is fine. The singing is good. But it is also good to hear some of the old Negro spiritual songs occupella, singing without music, every once in a while. You hear a lot of talk these days that preacher don't preach like they use to, and song not sung like they use to. Yet and still you get out of it what you put in. If you don't take the spirit to church with you, you sure can't get it out of the church whin you get there. In other words you build on what you take. You don't give nothing, you don't get nothing.

Sister Riddle baptise me whin I was about seven year old. About ten of us kid were baptise down on White Rock Creek on Doctor Dye place in a picnick place. Sunday School would last at least two hour. Then Mr. Bud Thorton would get up and talk a hour. Whin I was younger I all way thought he was a preacher. People would be driving by Preston Road and stop by. They would be white or black, and they would be from all most anywhere in the states. Of course, back then everybody would try to find a church to go to on Sunday, even whin traveling.

Some of the thing I can remember and never understood were that the men would dress up and go to church and stand around out side talking, and most would never come in church unless there were quartets singing. There use to be several quartets get together and sing against each other. Some would call it a contest. There were four of us boys about fourteen to sixteen year old and we had a quartet name the Rising Star Jr. The boys were me, Sonny and Willard Harris, and Henry Arnold. The older quartet were call the Rising Star Sr. Every where the older men would sing, we would too.

At the special service and revival the church was all way full. Most all the white folk that live out on the country would come to listen from time to time: the Haggards, the Pearsons, the Shepherds. Also other church from Rock Hill, Pilot Point, Frisco, and White Rock would participate with song groups and preaching. It would last all week to about twelve at night and all day Sunday.

Whin the preacher preach, you got to bear the preacher up and support that preacher. The fire ought to come from the altar. If the preacher build a fire in the pulpit, it reflect to the people in the pews and they respond. If he stir up no fire then he don't get no response from no body. They sit up like a calf looking at a new gate. A poor preacher if he had a stack of railroad ties with gasolene poured on still couldn't build a fire.

Of course some time the preacher get fired up and go on and on and on. Then some sister start humming and the people start singing till they sing that preacher down.

In pray meeting an old deacon or sister could get on their knees and pray all night. Some one might get happy and start shouting while prayer was going on. Some of these sisters or brothers could preach the gospel on their knees, yet you had to let them preach it out. If they was on ther knees too long, somebody started a singing to sing them up. You sing a preacher down from the pulpit, but you sing a deacon or a sister up from ther knees if they was on them too long.

121

If you would ask me my favorite verse I would tell you the 23 Psalm and the 133 Psalm. My young spiritual guiding and inspiration was my mother and my Preacher Sister Riddle. In later year and even today I go to my Uncle A. J. Stimpson for guiding and spiritual inspiration. I also stop by Mama Lettie Drake's and talk Bible. She is a great Bible student and very inspirational. I go fishing a lot and stay with my sister Ruth in East Texas. She has been a teacher in Sunday School and Church and is a great Bible teacher. She and I talk Bible every night on one subject or another.

And I pray to the Master Upstairs. I try to keep a telephone in my bosum and a hot line to Heaven. Bessie Lee, the rough and tough as boot leather younger sister, now work as a evangelist. Where she use to have to be watch around the clock, she now has some one else to watch over her. God In Heaven. We pray the Lord will annoint us all with his spirit.

Praise God

I think it would be very misleading to compare any religion service of today with a service during my growing up days or those year before my time. I hate to think about people of today that don't realize what a church service, funral service, or even a mid week pray meeting meaned in the days of the old. The hand clapping, the foot stomping, the shouting, and the Amen. Whin you put these together with the emotion, it only mean one thing: freedom from struggling all the week.

The best I can remember is sitting in the chorus and some sister begins singing a song. The spirit may move some one to start clapping ther hand and stomping ther feet. It won't be long whin the feeling would fill the church. The song and prayer and stomping and clapping together would be so beautiful, one would only no that God had release a band of angel swooping over the little Shepton Church while God himself move into the church.

Being young, it was hard to no why I and the other kids would find ourself clapping our hand, patting our feet, and even crying. As I grew older I under stood why. I can remember thing like this: Some one would say, I've sweat all the week in that field for that white man. Now I'm going to enjoy God Day. After sweating all week and blister in hand and feet, this one day I'm free to sing. I can clap my hand because I happy. I can stomp my feet because I glad. I can shout because I feel alive and don't have to worrie bout no body stopping me. This let all the last week burden out. I don't have to think bout famley problum. I don't have to worrie bout that bad field of cotton. And I don't have to worrie bout no body telling me what to do.

So in any service, high emotion could strike any one because of the problum they were having or had all that week. Some time you could leave after service and some one would say, I can go home and face the trouble now. God have lifted all my burden. I ain't gonner let the kid worrie me. I ain't gonner bother about my husband running around. And I show ain't gonner let that white man cotton field get me down.

These service may not effect one like it would the other. From time to time it could, but it sure could make every body go home feeling good. All that week you could hear some one say, Child, we sure did have good service Sunday. I can still feel it in my bones.

I can remember those old sister saying, Child, it not easy to go through what I went through this past week and not lose your religion, and that why I can feel like jumping and shouting Sunday.

I can look back and remember word like these coming from some of the old men and women. Saying, I've work all my life to raise my family, and now that I got a little some thing the white man want to take it away from me.

In my own life time it not hard to see what the old folk were talking about. You work and work like a slave. You don't get much pay for the work you do. Then you got to borrow money to keep your famley alive and kid in school. And whin you get sick or unable to use the muscles or stand on your feet all day, you are drop like a hot potato with out any consideration.

You might even look at the way thing are now. The rise and fall of the Black race. Every time there is an advance in one way there is also a fall back in another way. It not hard to realize whin you grew up seeing thing and live through the same thing. And remember why the old would say, I had hell all week, but the Lord knows I is going to prays my Lord Sunday.

It like the song: The world didn't give it (religion) to me, and the world can't take it away from me. I'm so glad man didn't make me, for he surely would forsake me. That why I'm so glad God made me and I can praise him whin I want to.

Funral Service

While I was growing up I never got to go to but three funral service. That was my grandfather, Miss Charity, and Aunt Emma.

I remember whin my Grandfather died it was four day before he was funeralise and buried. Practical every night some one would be by to sit up with the box. The box was all way in the largest room in the house—a bedroom. It was kept close during the day and open at night whin it was cooler and there were people there to fan the flies away.

The most remember thing I think about is the joy that we kid had being able to meet other kid from diffrent part of the country and city kid. The games we kid played may be the same as the one we normally had, but with new kid playing, the same old game had a lot more spices and pep to it. Not only that, we kid would run in and out of the kitchin snacking and peeping in the window to see what was going on.

As I sit and write this, my memory remind me that as I would be peeping in the window I see a cupple of people walking hand in hand or hugged up. It may be a friend or a relative, had not seen each other in years. As they walk up to the casket and look down on the face of the decease, ther face would light up, tears rolling down ther cheeks. But yet there were a beautiful smile on the lips. They would look around at each other and probly say, She or he look nature. I guess she or he is at peace at last.

And they would stroll on to the kitchin, sit down with some coffee, and chat about some old time they had together. All of this had to come from those old faithful one who beleave in God Word. You have joy whin there is death and cry whin there is birth.

The service were diffrent from that of today. I remember

funral service back then followed regular Sunday church service. Church service usual last to two or three o'clock. Then somebody say, We got to cut it short today; we got a funral service to do. There would be a few minute break and they would start the funral.

The box usual had been in place all morning. Depending on how well the person was knowed you could pretty well judge how long the service would last. Might last for hours. I think it was dark whin we got to the grave yard whin they buried my grandfather. If there was two or three preacher they preach, especial if the person was well known. Service were long but rewarding. After the service there were plenty of beans, chickin, cake, pies, home made bread, green potatoes, green beans, and peas. Every body eat.

I could never under stand why there were no moaning and groaning, hollering and crying. A funral service were a happy one. During the wake people talk about how good thing were and how good God is. Even though peoples no they would miss a love one, they feel that the dead were better off. I often hear someone say, That poor child work his or her self to death.

So the sad and happy would carrie over into the funral service it self: the songs that were sung, the pray that was said, or the words of Bible scripture the preacher said. What he preach about may spark a feeling that was more of a spiritual feeling from heaven than the sad feeling one had for the dead. Some time God spirit move in to the service like a shining lite, and people would feel more like the burden had been lifted.

In those days peoples sung, study the Bible together, pray together, and believe and fear God word. By being in a country community and knowing how the conditions was with each famley, it was easy to be together and happy about any situation.

During the wake people talk about how good thing were and how good God is. Even though peoples no they would miss a love one, they feel that the dead were better off.

Troubled Famley Down on the Farm

If you remember I talk about our family problm, especial between my father and my mother. I mention my visit to Sherman to visit my grandmother, Pearl Birks. That my mothers mother. At first it was maby once a month Dad would drive us up on a Sunday and spend a day or some time on Saturday and we all spend the night. Then whin I was about four years old Dad carried Mom and us kid to Sherman and drop us off. We stay three week or a month. I did not no why then, but talking to my sister Ruth it jot my remember.

My Dad was making boozes. He drink and chase women. My mother decided to seprate from him for a while and we went to her mother. We did not have much clothes, especial boy clothes. I wear dresses a lot after school to save my school clothes. There weren't many older boys in the naborhood, white or black, to give me hard time about clothes. So this is why and whin I started wearing girl dresses and no drawers.

Anyway we soon came home. I don't no if any thing were much better but mother stuck it out until I was seven or eight. Thing went hay wire again with mom and dad. This time one day mother sack up her and us kid few rag and caught the bus to Sherman. Dad was probly suprise to see us gone whin he come in from work. But by this time it made no diffrence with my mother. We kid didn't care. We were enjoying the visit and did not no why any way.

Dad would come visit pretty regular. We kid was glad to see him. He brought us food and a little money. Him and mom would talk a lot. After a cupple of month I guess Dad need us, especial the cotton need chopping and he had no help. So he finely beg mom back. We got back home and thing was pretty good. At least they stay until we kid were grown. Whin I was about seventeen they seprated again and this time for good.

128

Whin I was about seventeen they seprated again and this time for good. Mother put Dad out.

Mother put Dad out. But he all way come back. He had forgot some clothes or shoes. That was a way of getting back for a while. Some place to lay his head.

Finely in 1947 Mother pack all his clothes, sit them on the porch and whin he come looking for a place to sleep, she would not let him in. And in 1950 they got a devorse, but were still friends. I think they tried it again but it did not work. They stay in the same house for a cupple years but went ther seprated ways. Soon it was over for good. Mom move out to Dallas and went to work at the Baker Hotel. We all moved away. That was the end of all the famley problum.

If you think famleys only have trouble these day you are very wrong. Whin this type of problum happen in my young days, there were no money and you had to leave your food at home and go crowd in with another famley with no food. Nothing but the love of Mother and God kept us kid together and from starving. We were bless from Heaven.

Good Time and Bad Time

If you all way had a bad time you don't no how to appreciate good time, and if you all way had a good time you certain won't be able to handle a bad time. I can remember very well the good whin I was growing up. And that was whin the famley were all on one accord doing every thing together. That include from sitting down eating together to loading up in the car and going places. A famley that pray together stay together. Although Dad did not take part in our nightly prayers, he would be in the same room most of the time.

I can also remember those days whin bad times creep over, around, and into our house. It was like death was hanging around and sin had move in. Some time it may last a few day. Whin it did, my mother would tell me and my sister to go dig her some worm and catch her some grass hopper. Because, she would say, I got to get out of this house for a while. I'm going fishing. You kids can go, but I don't want to be bother with you cause I don't feel too good. This bad time usual came whin Dad and mom had a argument, a fight, but no licks were pass.

I don't no to this day what got into me once. One day I was about ten or eleven whin I tryed to stir up some trouble between Mom and Dad. I remember Mother would fix Dad dinner and send it to the field by me whin she was not working. One day while carrying lunch to the field, I thought up a lie and told Dad that Mom said she was tired of fixing his lunch. He sent word back and said, OK, but I put my word to it and said, Mom, Dad said you don't have to fix him a dam thing. He can cook his self.

Mom sent me back to the field and told me to tell Dad she would talk to him whin he got home. I again put my word to it and said, Dad, Mom said you don't even have to come home. She would rather not see you.

131

Although Dad did not take part in our nightly prayers, he would be in the same room most of the time.

It was about a hour or so before sun down. So Dad quit work and I rode to the barn with him. He started to the house and my butt start to get scared. I took my time behind him going to the house. I seen him go through the back door and a few minutes later he come out the back door with that big leather strap. Just as I come through the back gate and started around the house, he call me, Junior, and jump out of the back porch the same time, and I took off running around the house. I ran in the front door and run behind the door. Whin I run behind the door mom trap me and help hold the door on me. Whin Dad got there, the only thing he said was, Why did you tell them lies? And Mom said, Yes, Eddie Junior, why did you carrie them lies?

I no I was in trouble then. Mom release the door, and I no better than to run any more. So I did what I use to hear the old folks say—you might as well give God your soul cause your ass belong to him. I can tell you to this day, there were two thing I learn that day: Never try to make up lies, transport lies, or just plain lie. And I promise my self I would never do any thing to get a whipping like that again. Whin I think about that I can rub my butt and remember every lick.

I think some where and some time in every famley there is some good time and bad time. What we have to learn is no matter how bad the time are or what the problum is, there is a solution to it. But you got to work it out together. One person may have cause the problum but it take more than one to fix it. A little patience, a little Godly love, and a little praying will go a long way back to the good time.

A Lonely Mother with the Blues

It strange what people do and say whin the bad times come. I can remember whin my mother would get depress about no money, not much food, and my dad would not come home till late. She would start reading a while, walking the floor, cleaning up where she had all ready clean, humming a song.

Then she would go out on the porch and gaze out across the western horizon, and start singing, "Nobody Know the Trouble I See," and "In the Even Whin the Sun Goes Down, I Hate to See That Even Sun Go Down." She would just stand there looking at the sun. I guess us kid sense some thing was not right and no better than to bother her.

Soon she would feel better. If Dad had not come home, we would eat, and sit out on the porch until Dad come home or bed time. Then we had our Bible study, say our prayers and to bed.

Whin my mother would get depress she would start cleaning up where she had already clean.

134

Caring for Your Nabor

It hard to see why people do not look in on ther sick nabor. This day and time I've seen situation where Death in a famley next door to you in the city, and you won't no it.

Whin I was growing up, if word came that some one was sick, before the day was over nabor famly from the surrounding would go see what the problum is and see what the famley need, even bring the kids home and take care of them as if they were ther own, until thing got better.

Today if I would go next door or down the road to see how my nabor is doing, I might knock on the door and whin it open there might be a shot gun pointed at my head. I remember whin every body was a nabor, even a stranger. There were many day and night back in the country whin across the field a nabor or a stranger come by and got a meal and a night sleep. In this day and time you don't dare invite a stranger in to your home if you don't want to wake up dead. The next day or two your house would be clean out. We never fear this type of thing during my growing up days.

People just cared for each other back then. I guess it was because there were not much food in many famley and no money and some time no space for garden, or had space but no money to buy seeds to plant. I think people were more or less force into a position to help your nabor, help all you can in order that you may receive help. People in the country seem to have more love and Christ like humanity in them.

During the early forties and the war going on, people were able to go to McKinney to get releaf food: rice, bean, flour, and mostly food that would stick to your ribs. Along with garden, country famley made it pretty good. And it made no diffrence if you were white or black, country folk work together, eat together, and share hard time together.

135

Peoples would send ther kid to drop by at meal time. So mom and dad taught the kid whin some one come around to say, Ain't no body cooking around here.

I can't say much about the city folks helping each other. I no this because me and my sister were force to live in the city for a while and it was dog eat dog. And God for us all. There were few job and very little garden space to raise food. I can't remember ever getting full before bed time. There were never enough food and it was because city famley were larger. There were all way lots of grand kids left whin parents were sick or working. Also people hanging around.

If you were at a house whin it was eating time, you could pretty well eat, and you could bet your bottom dollar that whin meal time come some one was sure to show up. They probly smelt it. So peoples would send ther kid or even happen to drop by at meal time. It did not take long before Moms or Dads caught on. So Mom and Dad taught the kid whin some one come around at meal time to say, Ain't no body cooking around here.

What they did was go to the kitchin one at a time. Whin one come out of the kitchin they give a sign for another one to go eat. And this was going on in just about every body house in town. You had to stand guard over your garden, what little it was, to keep people out.

That the diffrence in city and country folk. City folk beg, borrow, and stole with no regard for ther nabor. Country folk feed any body came by hungry. All of this I've seen and heard.

Friends

During my growing up my mother taught us about friends. Even whin a stranger come to your house, treat them as a friend. She would all way say, Never turn down a friend or turn away a stranger. The one you turn away may be one of God angels.

During those early days my famley would meet at other one house at least once a month. Famleys would get together from miles around. If some one had no way to go, some body would pile every body up in ther car and off we go. We would sing, pray, play cards and dominoes, find out what each other needs were. If any body need food or clothes, they got it that night or the next day. One thing I remember about a good friend is they were all way there whin you need them. They were there, white or black folks, rich or poor. Friends were friends.

I had many good friend while growing up. Those who were closest to me, we stuck together no matter right or wrong. We spend the night together even if we had to walk miles to the other house. We fight together and we fight each other, but we protect each other. These I call day to day friends that soon fade away whin they famley move on to another area.

Another friend was a white boy name Frank Pannell. Still is a friend. Saturday and hollerdays and summer days whin we were not in school or working, we would get together and play, or go hunting and fishing. They stay down on the Harrington farm along Preston Road and we stay on Ray Haggard farm. He had a gun and I had a gun. So we would go hunting, kill rabbit or squirrel. And then we would split them up. He take half and I take half. We once climb a tree and capture three baby squirrel. He keep two and I keep one. We brought them home and feed them bottle milk from the cow. Finely I gave my one to Frank and he raise them and keep them for I don't no

Another friend was a white boy name Frank Pannell. We would get together and play, or go hunting and fishing.

how long. He is still a lover of small animal.

Because in my growing up days there just weren't that many boys around where I lived, I hung around grown up men a lot. My cousin Almond Drake was older than my dad and never did marry. He live with Uncle Ronney and Aunt Emma all his life. I would think he was a lonely man. We became attach to each other as we work together and I spend a lot of time with him in the field driving his team while he pull corn. We become like a older brother taking care of a young brother. By the time I was eleven or twelve, I move in with him. He cook and clean. And he carrie me every where he went. I stay with Tank until we move away from Ray Haggard place and then almost every Friday night he pick me up and I spend the week end with him until I went to the army.

As a boy I got to know some of the land owners I work for

on the west side of town. Whin I left for the army at eighteen year old, I had no idea that some twenty-five or thirty year later whin I return home as a sargeant, I would become involved with the same men. As a man I was able to go one on one with them and we were able to understand each other feelings and needs. Life gave me a chance to no how they felt about me as a black man as well as me about them. I grant you all men were not as easy as some. There were still that superiority some had in ther heart that being Black was still under that slave mentality and no matter what you did, if you were white, you were right; if you were black, get back. And there were some just as eager to see you get ahead and have a fair share and were willing to do more for the Black if they could, only to find out that if they did they would become an out cast within famley and other peers.

Then there were some men that I and them got close enough to each other we were like brother—men like Willie Carpenter and John D. Wells. These were a special breed of men, especial to me. I shall write about these men and tell what feeling we had for one another as a black and a white man. I hope some day peoples will understand that time, places, peoples, and the inviroment changes and it up to each individual to search ther own heart and become a part of this world that God has made for all men equal. This is my own opinion about what I feel about these men and the life we share together.

I look on Ray Haggard as a head em up, move em out cowboy who sat tall in the saddle as he rode his horse Robbin. He was a farmer as well as a horse, mule and sheep breeder. He raise my dad from twelve year of age and gave him twelve acres for share cropping. He was my famleys source of survival. To me he was all way a welcome site whin he would ride up or drive up to my house.

Ray cared for folk. We may not have had stake and potatoes every day, but he made sure we all way had some bean, flour, and meal in the kitchin and I'm thankful to this day for men like Ray back in those days.

John D. Wells was a man I may not be able to put down on paper the way I feel in my heart. He was a father to the fatherless, he was a mother to the motherless, a brother to the brotherless. He could make you sad with tears at some thing that had happen and he could perk you up whin you were low in spirit with just one or two word.

I met John as boy whin he gave me a job in order to help ends meet for my famley. Later he gave me a job as a man because he trusted me to do the work he needed did. We share many hour together riding up and down the road and on rainy day whin I could not work the field I would drop by the office and we would talk. Every time we have a long talk the name Willie Carpenter came up because John grew up with Willie and by this time I had a strong relationship with him too.

John all way make sure you had plenty of food to eat. And he would fix food and bring it to the field to you. He all way ask me how was my famley doing and especial how was my Dad, Pete, doing. He all way had fruit for you at Xmas and on hollerday he would all way say to me, Have you got enough food? You better take off and spend the hollerday with your famley. And he would all way tell you to go to church if you want, even whin we would be bog down and behind in the farming. John was the type of man that had the gentleness of a mother hen with all her bittie chicks, yet he was a man like a stone monument.

Willie Carpenter was one of the most influential men in teaching me about farming after I come out of the army as a sargeant. And after teaching me, he and I set down to his dinner table and over a shot of whiskey he said to me, Sarge, I think I'm going to retire and I want you to run the farm and take care of the hogs. This responsibility gave me the incouragement to learn more. I learn about hog marketing, grain and cotton marketing. I would keep books. The only thing Willie would tell me is where to plant and how many acres to plant. There were three peoples I would go to. If I want to know about hog, I go to Pat Cothes. If I wanted to no how much fertilizer to spread or seed to plant, I go to John Wells. Whin I need some help to work the fields, I go to my dad.

Willie was a friend and he would back you up as long as you were right. He did not see any color barrier. I never heard any racial slurres come out of his mouth. I did see him get angry at some one whin they use the word nigger. Frank's girl Elizabeth all way had girl come out to visit. One was John Wells daughter Sarah. During summer months and just about all hollerday there were four or five girl running around the barn in the hay loft. Willie would all way tell me, Sarge, keep an eye on them gals in case they get hurt.

He had some of his friends over one day and Willie and them were all getting ready to leave. I was out in the shop. He told me where they were going and he would not be back for a while and told me to keep an eye on them gals, and his friend made the accusation, You mean to have that nigger watch over them white girls? Willie got angry. Said, You dam right. I trust Sarge to take care of any thing I got. So he told them they could go with out him. He just soon not go with a bunch of fool like that. And that put a seal and bond tie with Willie and I.

There is another thing Willie would do. He tell me whin I got ready to go fishing to take off. If I ever got sleepy or felt bad while working, find me a shade tree or knock off and go home. He and I would all way go hunting the first two or three days of dove season. This was good old Willie.

Miss Ammie Wilson was a strong hard core woman who had

some thing else going for her. She was a beautiful woman. But she did not let the beauty go to her head. You would have to look into her eyes and see the smile on her lips only to feel that behind those eyes and under neath that smile and down under neath that beauty, she had kindness, she had love, and she had care and concern about the peoples she came in contact with.

My mother was house cleaning for Miss Ammie with her friend Warnita who was with child. I drop by one afternoon after school to see Mother, and Miss Ammie was telling my mother she could not get any help. I ask her what kind of help she need. She said, I got farm work to do. I got a tractor that won't run and no body to fix it. I ask her to let me try to make it run. She said, Have at it. I walk out in the field where the tractor was. It was park about the same spot where Wal-Mart is now. The tractor was a Molene. I tinker with it until I got it started, look it over good, got a feel of this type of tractor, and began to plow. It was a three disk braking plow. I plow the rest of the day.

The next morning by sun up I had fill the tractor up and was plowing. I don't think she no that I was plowing for a day and a half. She walk out across the plow field, stop, put her hand on her hip as if to say, I just be dam. Anyway I finish up that field, come to the house, we sit down, had some thing cold and some cookies. Then she begin to tell me about her self and her sheep. Here I am, a seventeen year old boy and she would say, The Lord is sure good to me. She told me to come eat dinner every day. If she was not there Warnita would feed me.

Then she said, Let go to the sheep barn. She begin to tell me ther name, how old they were, and where they had come from. I remember she pointed out a pair of Hampshire sheep and said, I just got them from Australia and they are my pride and joy. I ask her how much they cost. She told me and I let out a sound like wowee. I had all way been getting up early in the morning feeding the horses, cows and sheep whin we work and live on the Ray Haggard place. So I ask her did she want me to feed her sheep. She turn and look at me and said, Hell no. No body feed or fool with my sheep but me. And that was that. No question ask.

Then she want to no about my schooling. She incourage me to get all the education I could. She would give me and keep me with a job, but don't skip school for work. I work for her about two year. She often praise me for my work and said I was the only one she could get any work from.

She was the one woman whin I got ready to go to the army, told me, I would like to keep you but where ever you go or what you do, do it the best way you no how. And continue to get an education. She was a strong woman and was willing to give a person a chance to make something out of them self, black or white. While I was in the service she would all way send a hello by my mother and wish me well, and whin I came home make sure I visit her. I would drop by and see her whin I come home. We would have coffee or tea together and she would fix me a dinner.

I have no regrets about meeting this woman who kept her beauty hid under a straw hat tied down with a scarf, wore riding britches and carried a short whip. A woman of courage and compassion, yet a very strong and demanding woman who could touch your life in a way you could not help from loving. This was Ammie Wilson.

In recent months I think the closest friend I meet was T. V. Drake, son of Uncle Devil Horse. Knowing him all my life and a cousin, but in just recent years he and I become just like brother. We went to church together, we talk about farm and city life, and we work together researching information for a very memory cause: a state marker for Shiloh Baptist Church 100th birthday with the help of our friend Mrs. Frances Wells, who has become a very close friend and a willing worker for a great cause. Without Mrs. Wells help I would still be struggling trying to do what I'm doing now, writing up this remembers of my self. Where else can you find a friend who will take time out for something such as this. T.V. thank her and I appreciate and thank her.

Bonnie and Clyde

As I look back at the first little house I was born in, I remember it was located down behind trees and along a creek, hid from the outside world. Whin I was about three or four we got word from Ray Haggard that we could move into the Big House. This is where mother said, A home at last! But this home become more than just a home. For my famley it also become a motel from time to time and a cafe most of the time.

Now for you reader, let me see if I can paint the pitcher I'm telling about. I remember that during the thirties and the Depression, every where you go peoples were doing a lot of traveling going to and fro, here and there. Some walking or hoboing, some horse and wagon, some car, and some riding the bus. I suppose looking for a better place than the last.

Now pitcher this: You are traveling along a Texas hiway, Preston Road. You are hungry and thirsty, tired of walking or having trouble with your car. All of a sudden you top the hill and as you come to the start of the curve and down the hill, you see a big two story house off to the right front of you down about seventy-five or a hundred yard. A road lead off the hiway down through a paster to the house. You might see some one stirring around and you may not. There is no signs posted and the house look as if it have big welcome across the front, so you walk slowly or drive slowly down the trail to the house. Whin you get there some kid run out waving and speaking about the same time. A little short, plump woman or a six foot slim man come out on the porch. This was mom and dad. One of them would say, You look tired and thirsty. Come on in and rest a while. I'll get you a drink. Are you hungry?

Some time it may be one person, some time two, or a car with a famley. It made no diffrence who it was or how many it was. You could all way get a drink of something cool and a meal before you go—even a night rest if you want. From the day we move in that big two story house around 1933 until about 1944, there were all way some one stopping by. I think the location of the house and the beautiful site to look down at from the main road and the entrances and exits it had were a welcoming site.

The next episode is a little fuzzy because during these same years we had a cupple of visitor to stop by one after noon before night. They were like any body else passing by but dress a little diffrence and had a better looking car. I never talk about these folk or thought about them because as a kid we were told to keep our mouth shut and we aint seen nothing! I can remember that evening we had another old man visiting us. Of course, he was like the famley. He came by every week end, and every time it come a shower of rain you could look up and see Mr. Hen. He know this cupple who stopped by, and being the type of man he was, he ask the cupple, Aint you Bonnie and Clyde?

There were no respond. Any way it was about night and we all ate supper. After supper Mr. Hen said, Well, I hate to eat and run but I got to go and feed my mules. Clyde ask daddy if he had a radio. Dad all way keep some type of radio. The two borrow the ear phone radio of Dad and said they would like to rest. So Mom fix my bed in my room and gave it to them. They told dad and mom they had to move on some time that night, so whin I woke up the first thing I did was go out front and look for the car. They had gone.

For about cupple of days I think we become the most popular black family in Collin County. There were peoples from every where stopping by. From riding horse back to driving Cadillac, white and black, police and state trooper like wise. Every body had question. What did they look like? What were they wearing? Did they have guns? Where did they sleep? What did you feed them? How long they stay? Did you get scared?

One of the main question was, How much money did they

give you? No body never did no that. Dad and mom use to talk and tell people years later about Bonnie and Clyde. Like I said, I guess I was grown before I ask Dad or Mom about that episode. They had follow ther action since that night. The famous bank robbers, who may have been bad news for the bankers but was good news for this famley, that evening that Bonnie and Clyde spent with us.

Millie and Ed Diner

Whin I began to write this story, I was thinking and often wonder, Would any one or any body be interest in what really happen to black famleys during the 1930s whin the Depression and dust bole? I thought my grand and grate grand kids might read a history book some day and would like to no what happen and how we made it through the thirties out on a farm ten miles north of Plano along Preston Road in Collin County.

Up until this day and time I've been through one Depression as a young boy who no how good gravy and home made biscus was. Down on the farm it was not about what or who you were, it was all about who had what and how much who had. I can remember very well what was in our kitchin or out in the garden, and chickin and turkey in the yard. I also can remember during those years of Depression, my home were like a farm house cafe the way folk would come and go or stop by and get some syrup and bread or a bowl of beans.

I remember a bus with about fifteen peoples on it turn over right at our gate where we turn onto Preston Road. It was about 1937 and the ground was cover with snow and it was cold. About 9:30 or 10:00 one night a knock on the door came. Dad answer and there stood a white man. Dad let him in, and he told us his bus had turn over but no body was hurt. So Dad went back to the bus with the man. And boy, was mom scared that the man was lying, and she really just did not no what to do. She got the gun and load it, huddle us kid in a corner, and watch the door, turning out the light. She said, I guess Eddie is OK. I don't hear no shooting.

Dad all way carried his pistol with him. Any way, a few minute later we hear a lot of talking. Then the knock on the door and a call came: Millie, open the door. It me—Eddie!

The door open and in walk fifteen white women and men,

half frozen to death. There were two or three kid and a baby. Mother started throwing more wood on the fire. Dad put a big pot of coffee on the living room stove. Mom went to the kitchin and got the cook stove going. By the time every body got warm, mom had the table set with egg, bacon, dry salt, sausage, and biscus. They all ate and Mom begin to place every body in a sleeping place. The kid pile in the bed with us, two or three men in my bed, and women in bed with mother. The rest sit up all night nodding in chairs.

Dad kept the fire and coffee going all night. The next day brake, Dad got out and caught a team of horses. He and the men went to set the bus back on the road, come back to the house, and ate breakfast. They took up a collection for Mom. The bus driver paid Dad twenty-five dollar and they left.

The reason I put this story here is to point out that mother never turn any one away from her door, especial whin they were hungry. And this is why I can give my mother and father high praises for being good providers. So, during the Depression we had and we gave. Because dad didn't mind wrapping his holey boots with grass sacks and tromping out in the snow to kill some bird or squirrel or rabbit. Dad didn't mind getting out and plowing in the freezing weather to make that dollar to pay for flour and meal to be ground for food. And Mom was no diffrence. She didn't mind wrapping us kid up and go scrap the little cotton left on a burr, or walking for five mile to do house work for a cupple of doller.

So this is why we as a famley during the Depression was happy. I really consider those were some of the best day of my growing up years. Remember, there were no money during the Depression, but you don't all way have to have money to help some one or take a can of food to the give away food bank at church for Buckner's Orphans Home.

Time were tough for many farm and city people, but it was

peoples like mom and dad that kept a lot of people from getting "miss meal cramps." So I don't doubt that some where on that road to glory you might see a sign say:

Millie and Eddie Diner
Open around the clock

Menue for today
Breakfast
Bacon or sausage
Gravy with homemade biscus

Lunch
Red bean with fat back
Corn bread

Dinner
Black bird dumplin
Or rabbit stewe
Corn bread

Just a thought

One of the thing people offen over look is yesterday years. If one would only stop to think how did my old fore father and mother make it. You must remember all this concrete, fine home and shopping mall was once all dirt field, stream, river, woods, briars and meadow. Famley had to make a living some kind of way. All the wild animals were disappearing so clearing the land to grow food was a must for famley survival. Every famley in this world come from a famley who had to make ther living doing some odds and ends, from a little shop on a corner or digging in the dirt as a farmer. One thing for certain every thing you eat come from some kind of farm. Every thing you wear come from a farm, no matter whether you are white, black, red, yellow, whatever. Your fore father work hard and died poor so you can have what you got now.

As I sit here and ponder over the thing I've wrote and try to remember some of the important thing I may have forgot, I can't help to feel a little sad about sevral thing. My ancestors left no written records—just a few stories that are still remember. Remember that the days I would ask my dad and mom about their parents and there growing up days, they could not tell me much.

Although during my growing up days it was pretty tough to survive, yet it was still easier than what I would hear about how my grand parent and even ther parent suffered. Not only from the blistering sun, and the hour from dark to dark, with little food, no bed to lay in, no stove to cook on, no clothes to mount to any thing, no doctor, and on top of all this, some one standing guard over you with a whip in one hand and a gun in other, day and night.

I can see why some one would start singing, No body no the trouble I see, or way in the night one could hear some mumbling and sniffing and in the morning the pillow would be wet with tears. There is a song to fit that subject: In the midnight hours my pillow was wet with tears. Jesus came along and wipe away all my fears.

The old folk did not care to discuss or remember or talk about the painful memories because of the blood and sweat and over all living conditions. Some were good, some were bad. Back in my mind I can hear and see what my grand parent told me. I can see whin a rain come and it was too wet to go to the field. Children would be playing, women would be washing and men would cut wood, help hang out clothes and get the fishing pole and dig some worm, kill a chickin for the guts to use as fishing bait. By noon the clothes out on the line, the bean and bread is done, and some one would holler and say, Hurry up and lets go before the boss man come by and find something to do, and off to the creek to try to catch some fish. One thing about it—what ever was caught that day, whin they got back that night from fishing, they were clean and cook.

The thing I'm trying to point out that make me feel sad, there is nothing that I no of that can bring back those remembers—only what I heard my grand parent talk about. This is why I have written my own story. My spelling is bad, my hand writing is bad, and my language is bad. But my remembers is still in tack.

I think it's a pitty and a shame that this day and time, grown up and kid of the black race don't no where they come from and how they got here. Even my kid don't believe I had to wash and iron for house rent while growing up, or chop cotton with blister in hand or pick cotton until you can't stand up and knees so sore you could not crawl on them. I don't want to go back, but I don't want to forget where I come from. The truth is, only the Grace of God got us where we are now. The saying today for those who remember is this:

From no money to a bank account.
From no shoes to a change of shoes every day.
From no clothes to plenty of clothes.
From a wagon to a car.
From beans and potatoes to stake and gravy.
From a barn to a house.

Now if you think God ain't good, you better stop and look at what you got today because tomorrow is not promise to you.

I'm just a no body, who knows some body that can help every body. I would like to think that some day some body would ask Where is that book that a no body wrote? And some body will say Look on the book shelf and find *My Remembers*.

What I'm trying to say to the world in this writing, be you white, black, red, or yellow, you may have it made this day and time but some one had to suffer some where in the past to get you where you are today. Don't be too quick to say, I got this and that by my self. No, you did not. You got what you got by some one else sweat and blood and because God is good enough to loan you what you got. I'm no saint and I'm no preacher, but you would have to live through some of these thing to understand.

If you have any faith and believe in God, it is time to live it. You certainly don't have to advertise because if God live within you, your life is like a light in the dark. So don't be dismay. Heaven is there to stay. God is blessing you each and every day. Amen. Amen. Amen.

Closing letter to my grands and your grands and there grands

Now that you have read my letter I truly hope that you have some light about how your fore family lived. Try to learn some thing from your fore parents lives.

I remember as a boy I look at the stars hanging in the sky and hope and wish that some day I would be a shining star in some bodys life. That was a long time ago and the stars are still hanging. But as I look at you, my grands and your grands, I count each of you as a star.

I'm growing old. My grands and your grands may be here in Collin County where my life begin and will probly end, or may be on the other side of the world. Wher ever you are, I want you to remember that life is sunshine and storm. In the time of our prosperity, whin the skies of life are clean, the warm sun of friendship open, and the buds of the flowers bloom along

155

our path way, this we love. But we some time forget where all this beauty come from. We also need the strength-giving storm and showers to develop the beauty. Whin the storm of our life is in a turmoil, we only have to look at what God told Paul in 2 Corinthians 12:9. My grace is sufficient for Thee. For my strength is made perfect in weakness.

If we had not love one another during the tough time, we would not be able to look up and count the stars. But the strong love we had has made you a shining star that can be shared with others. All you have to do is look back and see where you come from in order to appreciate where you are today. We can see and read about stars falling from the sky. But I thank God that during our ups and downs He did not let us fall. Just remember, if love did it once, whin tough time come, love will do it again.

Remember grands, you and I have come through some tough time together. Every now and then your grands and there grands may also suffer some tough time. But you must remember all is not lost. Where there is prayer and love there is strength. St. John 13:34. A new commandment I give unto you, that ye love one another; as I have loved you, that ye also love another.

If you remember this I think you will have a sweet and full-filling life. As long as I live you may always feel free to come to me. I close with all my love.

Eddie Stimpson, "Sarge"

Appendix A

Family Tree

Great-grandparents	Clement Bell, b. in Kilgore, Texas
	Maureen Bell
	Andy Drake, b. 1833 in Alabama, d. 1933 in Plano, Texas
	Easter Drake, b. 1851 in Kentucky, d. 1934 in Plano, Texas
	Mose Stimpson, b. April 1830 in Tennessee, d. 1930 in Plano, Texas
	Millie Stimpson, b. June 1866 in Virginia, d. 1934 in Plano, Texas
Grandparents	George Stimpson
	Corrie Drake Stimpson
	Webb Birks, b. in Sherman, Texas, d. 1935
	Pearl Bell Birks, b. 11-19-1888 in Kilgore, Texas, d. 10-11-76 in Dallas, Texas
Father	Eddie Stimpson, Sr., b. 12-18-08 in Collin County, Texas, d. 1989 in Plano, Texas
Mother	Millie Mae Birks Stimpson, b. 4-28-14 in Forney, Texas, died 11-18-64
Sister	Ruth Stimpson Polk, b. 5-12-31 in Collin County, Texas
Sister	Bessie Lee Stimpson Dunbar, b. 8-28-33 in Collin County, Texas
Children	Wanda Jean Stimpson Jones, b. 7-9-51 in New Orleans, Louisiana

Grandchildren	Ivory Tyrone Stimpson, b. 4-3-57 in McKinney, Texas
	Donna Michelle Stimpson Okaro, b. 6-10-58 in McKinney, Texas
	Yolanda Renee Jefferson, b. 3-3-69 in California
	Katina LaShawn Henderson McQueen, b. 11-24-72 in California
	Ivory Tyrone Stimpson, Jr., b. 2-1-78
	Jeremy Stimpson, b. 1-25-83
	Jason Stimpson
	Todd Nicoles Stimpson, b. 2-23-89
	Chike Okaro, b. 10-26-87
Great-grandchildren	Eric Alexander McQueen, b. 9-18-95 in California
	Nekia Ann Morris, b. 8-28-91 in California

Appendix B

Stimpson and Drake Family Histories*

by Frances Wells

The Stimpson and Drake families make up a very important part of the black community in Plano, Texas. Andy and Easter Drake and Mose and Millie Stimpson all come to Texas from different states. Andy came from Alabama, Easter from Kentucky, Mose from Tennessee, Millie from Virginia.

Andy Drake was born in 1833 and died in 1933 at age 100. Andy married Easter who was born in 1851 and died December 1934. Andy and Easter had these children: Willie, Amon, Port, Lacy, Earl, Frank, Ronney (Ronnie), Cecil, Minnie, Bula, Lula, and Corrie (or Cary), Eddie Stimpson's grandmother.

Mose Stimpson was born April 1830 and died June 1930 at age 100. He married Millie, who was born June 1866 and died August 1934. Mose and Millie had nine children: Will, Rufus, Mitch Graylie, John, George (Eddie's grandfather), Mallory, Grady, Emma, and Maggie.

Two of the Drake boys married Stimpson girls. Earl Drake married Maggie Stimpson and Ronney married Emma Stimpson. Corrie Drake married George Stimpson.

These were among the first black families in Shepton and in the Plano area. Now they have all died and are only a memory. Uncle Andy and Aunt Easter, Uncle Mose and Aunt Millie—these name are well remembered in this community. In Plano we recently marked the graves of these patriarchs and matriarchs of the community.

Andy Drake lived on the east side of Preston Road and Mose Stimpson settled a mile and a half east of Andy Drake, just west of what is now called Coit Road.

Andy Drake worked two hundred acres west of Preston Road and Mose Stimpson worked two hundred acres east of Preston Road. The land they worked belonged to Silas Harrington, son of Alfred Harrington. Andy and Mose worked the land on the thirds and fourths, a responsible arrangement. They owned all the farm tools, mules, horses, cows, and barn animals.

The Drake boys did all the work on the farm until all married and moved away, some to town and some to Oklahoma. Andy Drake stopped farming in the early 1920s and he and Easter moved to town and stayed with his daughter Corrie Stimpson. He died in Plano in 1933. His wife Easter died there in 1934.

Mrs. Sallie Harrington set aside land to build a church. Before she give this land, the Drakes held church in the Drake home. When they began meeting in the church, they named the church the Harrington Missionary Baptist Church. When all the families moved away, the land went back to the Harringtons.

When the church would baptise it would be in the W. O. Haggard tank about a mile and a half west of the church. To get there they would use wagons and buggies. As new families moved into the community, the church would grow.

When Andy's and Mose's kids went to school it was in a building on the Huffman farm, north of what now called Park Boulevard. It was called Shepton School and Shepton Church. Shepton ran from the Shepard Ranch as far north as Clint and Clyde Haggard's farms. North of this was considered Lebanon.

It would be fun for the kids to walk to school four and six miles. The elder ones would have a chance to court. The school year began at the end of July or early August and then closed down after a month for picking cotton. Sometimes it was not open again until December or whenever the bad weather came.

In the spring if the weather was pretty, it was back to the field for some children who had to chop corn or cotton, but not for all.

When the school moved to the Harrington Baptist Church, it grew to the seventh grade. In the late thirties when families moved to other communities, the school closed, leaving the church to continue meeting for a time until it closed too. The place where the Stimpsons and Drakes lived is now covered with streets, homes, and stores.

But I can remember when Preston Road was not even called Preston Road very much. It was just a dirt road, a wagon and buggy trail. In the early twenties it was made a highway. They used mules to plow up dirt and make a bed with a dirt ditch on each side of the bed. They hauled red gravel from Camey Switch and dumped it on the bed. Each wagon hauled two loads a day. In the late twenties or early thirties it was black topped. From a trail to Highway 289 at the present time.

*Originally given as a speech in 1995, for Black History Month.

Index